WARRIORS OF WORSHIP

JIMMY MISTRI

BlueRose ONE.com
Stories Matter
NewDelhi • London

BLUEROSE PUBLISHERS
India | U.K.

For permissions requests or inquiries regarding this publication, please contact:

BLUEROSE PUBLISHERS
www.BlueRoseONE.com
info@bluerosepublishers.com
+91 8882 898 898
+4407342408967

ISBN: 978-93-6261-066-9

Cover design: Muskan Sachdeva
Typesetting: Rohit

First Edition: September 2024

BOOK 1

WARRIORS OF WORSHIP

Rayomand Artaxersis

CHAPTER 1

In a sleepy village nestled deep in the heart of the Bengal forest, a frail old priest sat cross legged on a crumbling dais. His flock, a pitiful and pathetic collection of the damned gathered around their spiritual leader. Each face reflected despair and disappointment, born out of the agony of their sorry existence. Each pair of eyes was pools of unshed tears, begging for salvation. The joyous occasion of Diwali was almost upon them. It was that time of year, when folks all over the length and breadth of India thanked Laxmi, the Goddess of wealth, for her blessings. She was the entity that ruled over wealth and prosperity. Each year she showered windfalls upon a chosen few. She chose who should receive and who should be denied. The entire country would soon come alive with glimmering oil lamps and noisy firecrackers. Mouth-watering sweets would be freely distributed among friends and families. For generations the old priest's flock were among the denied. They had to make do with homemade sweets made from low grade flour. While others prayed for wealth, the villagers prayed for salvation.

The plight of his flock immersed the priest in a state of despondency. He began to reminisce. The years rolled back to a time when he was a child, playing in the surrounding fields and meadows. At the time, the dais was an ornate piece of art. Priests, princes and peers gave stirring speeches on the principal aspects of life. Loyalty to God, king and country; charity and love were the main themes. The trees yielded more than enough fruits for men, monkeys and birds. The harvest each year was never less than bountiful. Joy and contentment dwelled in the hearts of every man, woman and child. Hunger and want were unknown. The entire village believed unwaveringly in the Supreme Being. The temple was the focal point of village activity. Children were lectured on the virtuous passages of the Gita, the Vedas and the Upanishads. The teachers enthralled them with tales from the Ramayana and the Mahabharata. It was a period of coveted prosperity. He felt blessed to have experienced the last few years of that glorious period. Yet he felt cursed to have witnessed its demise.

The wretchedness of their existence pained him. His eyes were resplendent with the wisdom of the ages. His face, wrinkled, motionless and serene, displayed none of the emotions that raged within. He knew well the reasons responsible for the miseries of his flock. Prosperity brought with it the curse of greed. It is Satan's tool to lure mankind away from righteousness. It corrupts the mind and the soul. Satiated by an endless source of wealth, the villagers at the time craved for the pleasures of the flesh. Avarice and debauchery became their creed. In time the satanic malady afflicted the vast majority. Religious rites were replaced by vile orgies and wicked revelry. Wenches were imported from nearby towns. The temple was converted into a tavern of transgression. Prayer books were replaced by obnoxious pornography. Holy water was replaced with alcoholic drinks. The rulers resorted to unreasonable levies, unprincipled demands and unjustified punishments on the devout. Women, girls and even young boys lived in constant fear of their debauchery. The priests who dared to openly defy their excesses simply disappeared. The devil reigned supreme.

Outraged, the Gods let the hammer of divine justice fall swift and hard. Year after year, floods, famine and pestilence ravaged the land. The productive paradise degenerated into an unproductive hellhole. Those with means fled to the cities, taking with them all the wealth, including the silver statue of the Goddess. Those who remained were reduced to a miserable lot of scavengers, subsisting on the meagre hand outs of Mother Nature. The priest knew that their redemption lay beyond such human sensibilities as pity. They were the victims of 'Karma', reaping the seeds of blasphemy sown in previous incarnations. He wondered if mankind would ever understand this. Or would it forever remain an enigma that would drive humanity to acts of desperation, born out of fear, futility and faithlessness. Karma was a difficult subject to explain. The burden of present existence lay so heavily on them that no one cared about the transgressions committed in past incarnations. The very concept of reincarnation was corrupted by the influx of western civilisations.

The troubled old priest sighed deeply, exhaling the frustrating futility within him. In a voice that cracked with age and emotion, he tried as best he could, to soothe and console. 'You must not let your misfortune diminish your faith in the divine. You must not abandon the hope for a better tomorrow. Faith and hope are the essentials that fuel human resolve. They help us endure the trials and travails of existence. They are the guiding lights that will liberate us from the dark abyss of the present, towards the glow of a brighter future. Without them, all of humanity would live in a perpetual state of chaotic anxiety. Suicide would be a commonplace occurrence. The flesh will turn to dust. It is the soul that will live on to fulfil its divine obligations.'

When his discourse ended, the fever of futility spread like an epidemic through the throng. All they had ever received as compensation were mere words. They had heard them all before.

The crowd broke up into small groups of distraught individuals, discussing their plight. The murmur of disconsolate desperation filled the air. Silently he watched the confusion. A tidal wave of despair threatened to drown and destroy their faith. For decades he had fought hard to try and keep the devil at bay. He was not ready to give up now. He held up his hand to quell the turmoil of desperation. The crowd fell into an obedient and respectful silence. 'Keep your faith and trust in God, not in me. This term of trial is a God given opportunity for atonement. It is an opportunity to cleanse your souls of all its past sins. There are no quick remedies or devious shortcuts to rid your souls of this self-inflicted misery. No one can evade its adjudication. If you attempt to evade your just retribution, it will follow you into every subsequent incarnation. Only when your atonement is absolute will your trials and travails end.'

The sun sank over the horizon. The lengthening shadows spread silently over the village, like a phantom river, bringing with it the blissful hours of slumber. The damned returned to their humble abodes. The creatures of the sun left the stage. The nocturnal denizens sang out their arias in this tragic opera of survival.

CHAPTER 2

John Travers was the heir apparent to one of the largest commercial establishments in the world. Each year he organised a hunt. This year he decided to include their families. They camped in the dense jungle of Bengal. Much against his wife Anne's better judgement, he had brought along his four years old son Christopher. Bunya, Christopher's native companion completed the Travers contingent. Bunya was born and bred in the forest of Central India.

Their departure out of Calcutta appeared more like the Israelite exodus than a holiday excursion. They camped at a pre-selected spot in the forest close to a babbling brook. At sunrise the men left the camp to brave the dangers of the jungle. The women and children were left in the care of two local hunters and a contingent of helpers. The women saw off their men amid loud cheers and jeers. The ladies spent the day playing card games, gossiping, supervising the preparations of meals and tending to the demands of their children. The children played noisy games, oblivious to the possible dangers around them. They seemed not to mind the constant harassment of mosquitos and other insects.

The men returned without as much as a rabbit to show for their troubles. They appeared sullen and downcast. The sun hung low over the western horizon. The women refused to let them live it down. One of the wives wondered aloud if this was the animal's day off. Anne urged the ladies to be tolerant. She reminded them that their husbands were bragging about was their expertise at treasure hunts. The vivid colours of twilight faded away. The sky hung over them like a black veil, adorned with millions of jewels. The nocturnal rhythms of the jungle rang out in the chill night air. The men sat around a crackling fire, imbibing, brandy; smoking pipes and discussing the day's failure. The women had retreated to the tents to put the kids to bed. The incessant squeaks and chirrups of a myriad of insects, the occasional wail of jackals and deep guttural growls large cats, added to the thrill of the adventure. A rustling in a nearby bush arrested the attention of the men. The hunters remained at the ready with their guns loaded. A gaur calf emerged from the bush and stopped. It seemed unsure what to make of the strange creatures that blocked its path. It was too young and inexperienced to associate humans with danger. It tentatively moved closer to sniff the strange creatures. The men were unsure what to do with the unexpected visitor. The thought of tender calf meat was an alluring temptation. But they knew that the ladies would jump down their throats if they harmed the helpless little beast. Suddenly, and without warning, a dark shadow the size of a hillock, burst out of the bush and charged at them with unnerving speed. Its head was held low; its huge horns pointed at them and its hooves beat a rhythmic tattoo on the ground. Their rifles exploded simultaneously. The charging hillock staggered and crashed to the ground with an earth-shaking thud. It lay lifeless a mere ten feet away from the fire. The women rushed out of their tents, shaken by the unexpected gun shots. The men, proud of their conquest, encircled the slain beast. One of them informed the ladies that a Gaur is the largest bovine in the world. The calf let out a mournful moo and timidly approached its fallen mother. It sniffed and nuzzled her dead body to urge her to stand. It appeared bewildered by her lack of response. Despite their efforts it refused to leave its dead mother's side. Without warning

Travers shot it in the head. A cry of pitiful protests from the women resonated in the chill night air. They verbally attacked John in unison. Anne was the most vocal of them all. Travers explained that the calf was doomed the moment its mother died. Nobody could have done anything to save it. It would have certainly fallen prey to predators sometime during the night. The predators would have torn it to shreds and possibly consumed it while it was still alive. It would have suffered a gruesome death. John's justification for his deed did little to console the gentler hearts.

A team of helpers carried the calf towards the pit of coals to prepare it for dinner. It took all the men in the camp to drag the cow away. Soon the air was replete with the aroma of tender gaur meat roasting over an open fire. The flames swayed in the breeze like phantom dancers, casting eerie shadows around it. Moths and other flying insects of all shapes and sizes hummed around the fire, as if serenading the dancing flames. Mesmerised by the glow, some of them flew into the flames. A host of carnivores were attracted by the aroma of roasting meat. Yelps, howls and growls filled the night air. The ladies sat close to their men, petrified with fear. A predator dragged the mother away. To assuage their dismay, Colonel Smith volunteered to relate a ghostly experience from his days in the army. 'Stop him before he bores us to death' one of the party commented. The ladies shushed the men and urged the colonel to relate his experience.

'It was a cold and moonless night. Kali, my man Friday and I were the only survivors of a vicious Afghan attack. In the deathly silence and blinding darkness we decided to make our way back to base camp. We could barely see the ends of our noses. We climbed to the top of a rocky peak. Only the sound of our breathing assured each of the others presence. We needed to feel around before taking each step. Suddenly, a shimmering apparition appeared out of nowhere. It was just a featureless female shape. It appeared to hover in the air. What puzzled me was that I could see her clearly when all else was cloaked in blinding darkness. The spectre seemed to be trying to communicate through frantic gestures. Kali, started to back away. He clutched my arm, shaking like a Parkinson patient. The apparition enfolded me in its arms, forcing me to stop.'

'Either it was wishful thinking or your man Friday was making a pass at you' one of the men said. The women begged them to shut up. Unfazed by the crude comment, the colonel continued. 'To my astonishment, she disappeared just as suddenly as she had appeared. There we were, only inches away from the edge of a cliff. The fall would surely have kill---.' Colonel Smith's unfinished tale ended with the sharp crack of a rifle. A dark stain spread across the colonel's shirt. He keeled over head first, into the camp fire. In moments the atmosphere deteriorated from a peaceful campfire gathering to a hell hole of madness. Hooded demons mounted on horses, burst onto the scene. They seemed to be everywhere, screaming like Banshees from hell. The men returned fire, but there were too many of the marauders. Bursts of gunfire, drumming of hooves, demonic screams of the marauders, mingled with cries of pain and fear of the campers, filled the jungle air.

The women ran to their tents to be with their children. Anne Travers grabbed her husband's hunting rifle and waited for any barbarian foolish enough to try and harm her child. Buniya placed his arm round Christopher's shoulders to reassure his terrified little friend. Anne was in a state of panic. She ran mindlessly into the midst of the madness. Christopher and Buniya stood by her side. She watched the carnage unfold before her. Amidst the madness, she noticed her husband fight his way towards them. He was only yards away when a hooded monster charged at him from his right. Turning and taking quick aim he fired, throwing the thug off his horse. A second mounted thug charged at him from the left, brandishing a shimmering sword. Anne screamed out a warning. John turned and levelled his pistol at the fiendish assailant. But the man and beast were already onto him in a flash. The assailant's blade whistled through the air and descended on him like streak lightening. It sliced his head clean off the shoulders. Anne stood dazed and motionless. She gaped mindlessly at her husband's decapitated head. She seemed oblivious of the danger all around her. She was unaware that death was closing in on them from all sides. Bunya had seen it all before. His village had experienced such raids on several occasions. He accurately gauged the situation and sprang into action. Lifting Christopher in one arm and dragging Anne by the other, he guided them into the pitch blackness of the forest. He pulled his mistress and companion down behind a large boulder. An eerie silence fell over the camp site. Bunya guessed the massacre had ended. Experience told him that the thugs had not yet left the scene. They were notorious for their greed of money, their lust for women and their compulsion to kill. He knew he must get Anne and Christopher as far away from the campsite as possible.

It seemed the entire forest had stopped to witness this macabre human drama. The silence was broken by the snap of a twig and the crackle of dried leaves. It sounded like a gunshot accompanied by castanets at a Spanish fiesta. Buniya realised a thug was on their trail. He gauged the thug's position and distance. The fiend was inching closer. Groping in the darkness, he found a sharp stone large enough to fit in the palm of his hand. He crawled to the top of the boulder. It felt like his face was pressed against a blackboard. A dark ghostlike form inched its way towards the boulder. His heart pounded, his pulse raced and his head throbbed. The thug stopped to get his bearings. Bunya leapt at the thug like a leopard. He hammered at the monster's head and face relentlessly with the stone. The thug, taken by surprise reeled under the onslaught. In the confusion his finger involuntarily pulled the trigger.

Startled by the deafening gunshot, flocks of birds, burst out of their roosts. Creatures big and small scurried away as fast as they could. To Anne's ears, the gunfire sounded like a cannon exploding in a cave. It shook her out of her trance. She grabbed her son and fled into the dense thickness of the jungle. She ran on relentlessly through thorny bushes, stumbled over stones, fell into ditches and collided with a number of bushes and trees. Her brain anesthetised by fear and panic, was oblivious to the multitude of cuts and bruises. She felt neither pain nor fatigue.

The dim glow of dawn seeped through the trees. She noticed a vast field, dotted with vaguely familiar shapes. It took a while to realise that she was looking at a cluster of huts. The huts represented safety for her and her child. She ran into the village, crying and screaming like a crazed animal. She collapsed at the foot of a crumbling dais, her son still clasped to her bosom.

Men, women and children rushed out of their huts, to investigate the obstreperous intrusion of their sanctum sanctorum. They stood huddled together, gaping at the alien pair. In the dim early morning light the colourless intruders appeared too ghostly to be human and too human to be ghosts. None dared to make contact, for doubts born out of fear of the possessed. The circle of villagers respectfully stepped aside when a frail old priest arrived on the scene. He knelt down beside Anne and gently stroked her hair. His touch traversed all barriers of culture and communication. Anne sensed that all was well and slipped into a blissful coma.

CHAPTER 3

The old priest chastised his flock for their unfounded fears. The villagers inched closer, one tentative step at a time. They dutifully carried Anne to the priest's tent. Christopher followed his mother, seeped in deep thought. The old priest treated his patient with prayers and poultices. Her wounds responded well to the indigenous treatment, but she remained in a state of comatose. The priest sensed that she needed more than homemade remedies. He dispatched a villager to fetch the missionary doctor. The days trudged by. Occasionally Anne would burst into an epileptic fit, thrash about uncontrollably; scream incoherently and slip back into a coma. This became a daily routine. The priest feared for his patient's life. He was in a race against time. The missionary doctor and the villager had not arrived. The old priest nerves were stretched to the limit. He believed the woman and child were sent to him by God. He was not prepared to let his maker down.

Getting any information from the child was futile. Firstly, there was the language barrier. Secondly, the child remained silent and unresponsive. He even refused to interact with the village kids. The priest worried for the child. The boy only ate a handful of sweet berries and drank a glass of milk. All day the child would sit in the doorway of the priest's hut like a forlorn puppy. He stared fixedly at the open field in front of the hut. Every now and then Christopher would mutter to himself in English and fall silent again. An abnormally oppressive afternoon had confined the villagers to their huts. The children were ordered to remain indoors. The priest busied himself with preparations for the evening prayers in his thatched roof hut. As usual, the boy sat silently in the doorway. The priest feared that the traumatic experience might have unhinged the child's mind. Suddenly Christopher stood up and craned his neck. He appeared animated. Through his aging eyes, the priest could only see a blurred expanse of land. Without warning Christopher darted across the field, running like one possessed. Fearing the worst, the priest shouted after the boy to stop. Frustrated, he shouted at no one in particular to stop the lad. In a state of confused agitation the old man followed Christopher as fast his aging legs would permit. He watched with dismay as Christopher crazily flayed his arms and shouted an unfamiliar name repeatedly. The old priest's frail condition forced him to stop and catch his breath. A hazy figure drifted over the field like a mirage. Both Christopher and the mirage appeared delirious with joy. It was like seeing Castor greet Pollack after a long period of separation. Once the insane ritual of their reunion ended, Buniya approached and paid homage. Later Buniya related their tragic tale. As if by divine ordinance, the doctor and the village lad arrived the following day. Anne, Christopher and Buniya accompanied reverend Pierotti to the missionary hospital.

The villagers returned to their pitiful lives of drudgery. They faced their trials and travails with mute acceptance. More than a month had passed without any word of Anne's condition. Six weeks later, Brother D'Cruz arrived at the village with news that Anne had been discharged after a full recovery. The old priest hurried to his tent to light a lamp of gratitude to his maker. Brother D'Cruz informed them that Anne and her family members would be visiting the village as soon as possible. That evening the old priest held an extended session of prayers.

****

For nearly a month the villagers waited in anticipation of Anne and Christopher's arrival. A pessimistic villager believed that the event was nothing more than a mere paragraph in the life story of the white lady. According to him, the brown people were nothing more than tools to be used in times of need. Most of the villagers agreed with the sceptic. The old priest was livid. He gave the pessimist a piece of his mind.

A week later, the peace of a sultry afternoon was broken by the distant rattle of approaching bullock carts. Six carts driven by a dozen bulls pulled into the village square. The sleepy village turned into a bustling hub of frantic activity. The curious villagers circled the caravan in anticipation of Anne's appearance. A welcoming cry filled the air as Anne alighted from the cart. She was followed by a distinguished looking gentleman, Christopher, the reverend Pierotti and lastly Buniya. For the villagers it was a momentous occasion. It offered them joyous respite from the monotony of life. Anne introduced the distinguished gentleman as Sir Phillip Travers her father-in-law. Brother D'Cruz, their interpreter stepped off the second cart. Once the hugs, handshakes and pleasantries were dispensed with, the villagers began the laborious task of unloading the carts. Generous portions of grain, pulses, clothes, blankets, cooking utensils and other essentials were distributed among the villagers. Toys, clothes and sweets were handed out to the children by Christopher and Buniya. The old priest reminded the sceptic that reward and retribution lay solely in the hands of The Lord.

The villagers plied their guests with gifts of berries, homemade sweetmeats and sweetened buttermilk. Anne explained to her father-in-law the immense sacrifices the villagers needed to make for those simple gifts. The old priest made preparations for a religious ceremony to bless Anne. Christopher presented the old priest with a gold pocket watch. The gift took the old priest aback. Accepting any gift for services ordained by the Creator flew in the face of the priest's moral and ethical beliefs. He stared at it for a long moment and said in a soft voice 'I cannot accept this, my son. My flock can barely manage to fill their stomachs. How can I accept something as valuable as this'? Sir Phillip intervened. He insisted the old priest ask for whatever he and his villagers need. The old priest stood in deep thought for a long while. Finally he asked Sir Phillip to restore the temple to its original state and install a statue of the Goddess Laxmi.

For nearly a year the village remained vibrant with the activities of masons, carpenters and artisans. A temple that had been converted into a tavern of transgression passed out of existence. A monument of architectural beauty stood in its place. The crumbling dais in the village square too had been restored to its previous glory. The old priest waited anxiously for the arrival of the promised statue.

Anne and her family returned to the village, bringing more gifts for the villagers. The air resonated with the thump of drums, the clangs of cymbals and the peels of bells. Men and women danced to the rhythm of the drumbeat. A chorus of women sang a medley of Hindu hymns. The children clapped, giggled and ran around senselessly. The following day the priests prepared for the installation of the statue. Sir Phillip, the reverend and the village elders sat by the entrance of the Goddess' chamber. Tradition dictated that Anne being a woman could not be present at the time of the ceremony. She would be represented by Sir Phillip and Christopher. Christopher bullied Bunya into sitting next to him. A junior priest objected to Buniya's presence.

Christopher threw a tantrum that stunned the junior priest. He stomped away indignantly. The little firecracker finally had his way. Buniya was visibly uncomfortable. The old priest noticed Bunya's discomfort and gave him a reassuring nod and smile. 'In the Goddess's eyes everyone is equal' the priest whispered. The men of the village sat behind the elders. The ladies occupied the rear end of the congregation hall. Anne insisted to sit with the ladies. Sir Phillip, Christopher and Buniya were ushered into the Goddess's chamber.

The tolling of the large silver bell heralded the start of the ceremony. The old priest commenced his chanting. Two junior priests joined him. From time to time, a shower of saffron coloured powder, grains of rice and multi-coloured petals rained down on the honoured guests. An hour later the chanting came to an end. The moment had come for Sir Phillip and Christopher to unveil the statue. A stunned silence fell on the proceedings. A statue of pure gold embellished with diamonds, rubies, sapphires, emeralds and pearls was revealed. Not in his wildest dreams did the old priest expect such a priceless work of art. Sir Phillip, Christopher, Buniya and the junior priests placed the Goddess on the marble pedestal. Anne and the reverend were the first to enter at the end of the ceremony. The rest of the village folk followed. They entered the chamber in pairs to pay their respects. Each one came away awe struck by the splendour of the statue.

CHAPTER 4

Sir Phillip Travers passed away four years after they returned to England. Since Christopher was still a juvenile, Anne was forced to learn the ropes of the business. For fifteen years she managed the business with creditable efficiency. However, she never forgot her debt to the old priest and the village folk. Every year she visited the village on the anniversary of the hunting tragedy. On auspicious Hindu holidays she made sure that her Calcutta office sent gifts for the villagers. She was in her late-forties when the crippling ailment rheumatoid arthritis rendered her bedridden. The debilitating illness prevented her from fulfilling her obligation to the villagers. When she passed away Christopher was left controlling the reins of the empire. He was still in his early twenties. His youth and inexperience compelled him to concentrate all his time and energy on the business. Thankfully he had an experienced teacher to guide him. The teacher, Sir Phillip's right hand man and confidant had been a loyal employee since before Christopher was born. Leisurely pursuits of youth were luxuries that had to be shelved. However, he yearned to visit the village and meet his childhood friend and saviour Buniya. Christopher could neither find the time nor the opportunity. Every time an opportunity arose, the pressures of business compelled him to postpone his trip. Three years after he inherited the multinational company, he felt confident enough to entrust management of the business to his senior staff. He believed they were capable and trustworthy enough to run the show. The time had come to return to India.

As the ship pulled into Bombay harbour, Christopher stood on the first class deck reminiscing. Memories of the horrific experience in the jungle came flooding back. He recalled his antics during the voyage. On his insistence, Bunya had accompanied them. At first Bunya remained tentative about going to a strange land thousands of miles from home. However, like everyone else he found it next to impossible to defy Sir Phillip's orders. 'You mustn't spend your entire life in a cocoon my boy' Sir Phillip said in his usual intimidating and authoritative way. 'Travel broadens the mind as much as books. Besides, it will be amusing to experience the oddities and idiosyncrasies of the so called superior English race.' They spent the days exploring the length and breadth of the ship.

The huge passenger liner announced her arrival with a deep resonant bellow. The air was replete with the sounds and odours peculiar to India. The cries of vendors and the din of the bustling crowds jolted his memory cells. He watched the scene with bitter sweet nostalgia. He recalled his mother telling him of someone who said that India was a land where he felt the pulse of God. Such profound philosophical sentiments were lost on him at the time. But now he could appreciate the depth of that man's perception. Maybe it was the mood of the moment, but he too felt the same way about this mystic land. Christopher walked through immigration and customs in the style esteemed dignitaries like him are accustomed. Junior dock officials ushered him through the crowd. He heard the public announcement system suddenly come to life. Whatever they were announcing sounded like garbled cacophony. But somewhere in the midst of incoherent gibberish, he distinctly heard his name mentioned. An army of staff members from his Bombay office rushed to greet him. A Hindu priest, accompanying the staff performed a brief welcoming ceremony. They exited the wharf in a group followed by a parade of coolies.

He was about to climb into his car when he heard somebody call out his name. The gravelly voice sounded vaguely familiar. He scanned the area, hoping to spot a familiar face. A man, waving frantically through the milling crowd caught his eye. The face brought back memories of his carefree days at Eaton. It was Robert Walsh, dubbed the Satan of Eton. After the exchange of pleasantries, Walsh insisted his friend join him for breakfast. He promised it would be an experience Christopher would never forget. 'You can forget about your Dorchester, George Cinq and Beau Rivage. This hotel stands in a class of its own. I am inclined to believe it was built during the reign of King Arthur. It has not been repaired or altered ever since. The dining room was salvaged from Rome soon after the city burnt down. The furniture originally belonged to the torture chambers of Torquemada. The menu would be rejected by prisoners from the middle-ages. One would find it difficult to guess if the eggs were fried or poached. The scrambled eggs were an Indian variant of Oliver Twist's infamous gruel. The buttered toasts are either too black and fragile, or too white and leathery. The coffee only looks like coffee. The tea is tepid water mildly coloured. If a person asks for marmalade or jam all he gets is a hearty laugh.'

Christopher was amused and intrigued. He agreed to join his school friend. At a glance Christopher saw that Walsh had not exaggerated. The Grand Victoria hotel was a rickety old wooden structure erected a bit over a century ago. The dining room which also served as a restaurant was dim and dingy. Paintings of plump women in varying stages of nudity, hung precariously on cracked walls of peeling plaster. Bent wood chairs swaying on their hinges, stood around tables draped with fraying and stained tablecloths. Customers were tucking into various versions of eggs. They were accompanied with lumps of flour that passed off as bread. The clientele comprised of the impoverished, the unemployed and the unscrupulous. They were the hotel's most regular customers. They came from diverse backgrounds. Bates and Spratt were once gainfully employed. They both came from respectable middle class families. However they suffered the unjust misfortunes that fate occasionally meted out to the undeserving. Bates' father was a protestant minister. Spratt's father worked for Her Majesty's postal service. Walsh was the son of a successful speculator. The speculator passed away when Robert was in his mid-teens. He found himself at the mercy of a social climbing tight fisted mother. Besides food, clothing, shelter and education, Robert did not receive a brass farthing. Robert rebelled by straying from the straight and narrow. He had never experienced a single day of honest work. His idea of gainful employment was to find ways to make a quick buck. The means to that end did not matter. He was known to have cheated the trusting, deprived the needy and landed the innocent in all sorts of trouble. For reasons known only to her, fate decided to thrust him into the lives of Bates and Spratt. They were now, like three peas in a pod. The pod was called the Grand Victoria hotel.

A collective intake of breath by the guests made Bates and Spratt glance at the entrance. Everyone's eyes were fixed on the aristocratic visitor. In this place, the presence of the likes of Dillinger or Jack the ripper would have gone unnoticed. However, Walsh's guest was a different kettle of fish. He was as out of place as a king at a beggar's convention. Bates and

Damien could not but feel pity for the unsuspecting victim. Walsh introduced Travers as his friend from Eaton. They both wondered what terrible fate Robert had planned for the aristocrat. Soon the atmosphere around the table turned cordial. While waiting for Walsh and his guest's breakfast to be served, they discussed politics and the possible outcome of the Great War. The topic turned from the war to the battles of life. Travers was the first to speak. He related his life story in detail, consciously omitting any reference to the statue.

George, Damien and Robert could scarcely believe that someone like Christopher would suffer such horrors. Bates was the first to relate his tale. His story started by declaring his love for his boss's daughter Rosemary. The girl's father rejected his proposal for marriage on the grounds that he was not financially worthy. Soon after, a colleague offered to include him in a shady deal. The deal promised to make him a rich man. However it entailed cheating his employers. For days he struggled between love and loyalty. His love for Rosemary proved too strong. He succumbed to temptation. The colleague turned out to be a double crossing swindler. The swindler not only decamped with the loot, but also left him facing the music. He had lost his job and his sweetheart. Bates followed a lead that brought him to Bombay. He searched every nook and cranny of the city, but the double crossing swine had disappeared without a trace. On a gloomy September morning he entered the restaurant for a bite to eat. The restaurant was packed to full capacity. He approached the only table with an empty chair and requested if he could share the table. The men graciously welcomed him. The hotel was destined to be his home away from home. Spratt invited him to share the room and rent with him and Bates. Regular customers of the hotel referred to them as the curious trio. The booming voice of Walsh rang out loud and clear. 'Love be damned' Walsh said. 'The bottom line is that you proved you are a damn fool. In any transaction, if you are cheated because you did not play your cards right, it is entirely your fault. In my opinion you did the right thing by accepting the colleague's offer. But then you displayed your inherent stupidity by permitting him to dictate the terms. You should have insisted on mutually acceptable terms. Always keep in mind that the only person a man can fully trust in the world is himself.'

Damien Spratt used the opportunity to vent his frustration. He passionately condemned the female gender. He opined that the bible proved the first anti-Christ was a woman. Spratt's bitterness and aversion for women took everyone aback. His friends vociferously opposed his views. Spratt related his romantic experience that nearly put him behind bars. He was sent to India to reverse the losses incurred by the Bombay office. He soon realised that the office was riddled with incompetence. He was forced to dismiss several members of the staff. Among them was a cargo supervisor named Arun Rao. As days went by, Spratt fell madly in love with his secretary Rosie Jones. He declared that she was the most beautiful the world had ever seen. The beauties of history and the silver screen were hags compared to her. All his advances were met with lukewarm response. A day before Christmas holidays commenced, she presented him with a stack of papers to sign. As she leant over him, he could feel her soft thighs pressing against his shoulder. Inebriated with passion, he pulled her onto his lap and began to fondle her. Rosie responded with equal fervour. She agreed to shift their amorous liaison to his residence. He hurriedly signed the letters without reading a word. On the way Rosie doubled up with stomach cramps. He had no choice but to escort her to her home. Spratt never saw his love again. She had gone missing. The police suspected him of foul play. They accused him of using Rosie to misappropriate a large sum of money and then murdering her. It turned out that among the pile of letters was a cheque for ten thousand rupees. Months later the jury returned the verdict of not guilty. Recently an office colleague informed him that Rosie had acted to avenge the sacking of her paramour Arun Rao.

Walsh flatly refused to relate his life story.

CHAPTER 5

Friendship blossomed between Christopher and Walsh's companions. Spratt and Bates were offered employment in his Bombay office. Walsh was chosen to be his personal odd jobs man. They were all given expense accounts according to their respective salaries. Christopher insisted they accompany him on a trip to a village in Bengal. They were made to take an oath that what they saw and experienced would never be revealed to anyone.

Christopher's send-off committee descended on the station en masse. The train set off on its journey with a sigh and a jerk. It chugged through the urban jungle at a leisurely pace. Fearless men, women, children, stray dogs, cattle and goats defiantly crossed the tracks disregarding the danger. The city offered a panoramic view of factory chimneys and poorly maintained buildings. The train gained momentum as soon as it left the city limits. They sped past paddy fields dotted with quaint little huts. Village children joyously waved them on. Cattle gazed stupidly at the speeding beast. Dogs barked and ran alongside, in an attempt to chase the monster away. Soon the steam engine moaned and groaned as it climbed steep rugged hills. At times the wheels passed precariously close to life threatening precipices. The picturesque view enthralled Christopher as the train passed through pristine forests.

Christopher insisted on sampling the local snacks at every stop, despite Spratt's warnings. The temptation of unknown flavours and aromas were irresistible. He would invite the adolescent vendors into his compartment and shower them with generous amounts money. Christopher's low life guests upset the stuffed shirts in the first class compartment. One stuffed shirt voiced his disapproval in a raised voice. 'I say young man, if you are trying to impress us with your cheap display of wealth and compassion, it is not working. For the past so many hours we have endured the smells and sounds of these peasants infesting the cabin. We can take it no more.' The condemnation of the underprivileged children brought out the worst in Christopher. His face turned a cherry red hue. His eyes flashed fury. He spoke between clenched teeth, with a menacing tremor in his voice. 'This country rightfully belongs to them. It is their Motherland. If you are so offended by them, why don't you return to your precious England? God knows you and your kind have heartlessly exploited them for nearly two centuries.' Christopher's accusation prompted unanimous disapproval from the rest of the passengers. Another passenger threatened to inform the higher authorities of his anti-English attitude. Christopher told the man to tell whom so ever he wished that he Christopher Alfred Travers sided with the natives. The name created a stir in the compartment. For the rest of the journey they endured Christopher's roadside invitees in respectful silence.

The passengers changed trains at Baroda and then again at Delhi. The steam engine charged across the central plains at breakneck speed. Vast fields of wheat and paddy stretched out as far as the eye could see. The fields gave way to dense forests. Christopher enjoyed every minute of the journey. It was an adventure that would stay with him for the rest of his life. Walsh on the other hand was dissatisfied with everything. He complained about the food, the weather and a myriad of inconveniences. He never really cared much for nature and rural sceneries. The train screeched and sighed to a halt at Calcutta's Howrah station. The following day Christopher excused himself to attend to some personal work. He headed straight for the shop of his childhood friend, Buniya.

CHAPTER 6

Senior constable Kamalbir Singh strode through the marketplace, keeping a watchful eye on the activities. Since he was stationed here, the area had morphed from a melting pot of crime to a peaceful neighbourhood. At times, he needed to deal with pickpockets, shoplifters and cat burglars, but those were the worst of crimes.

The dons of the area found their spurious incomes steadily dwindle. The chief don of the area felt his grip on the residents diminish. He issued several threats and warnings to constable Singh. Kamalbir Singh considered the don nothing more than a pesky stray dog. The don bribed corrupt government official to have the constable transferred. His attempts were all in vain. The law abiding residents of the locality made a collective plea to the governor for Singh's continued services. The menace of the dreaded constable continued to plague the local underworld. Finally the don decided to confront Kamalbir on his own. He sent an anonymous letter to Kamalbir, threatening the lives of his family. A threat to his daughter was more than Kamalbir could bear. The tension started to tell on Singh's mental and physical health. He decided to walk his daughter to school and back every day. But the threats continued.

After considering several options, Kamalbir decided that the only permanent solution was to confront the don. He marched up the steep flight of rickety stairs. On the uppermost floor was a door painted black, adorned with a red skull and crossbones. Kamalbir knocked several times. No one answered. He kicked the door open. His large regulation shoe splintered the aging wood and undid the bolts. Three young lackeys were playing cards and guzzling beer.

They sprang to their feet shaken by the sight of the dreaded constable. They stood in one spot and gaped. The first to recover lunged at the policeman with a knife. Singh seized his wrist, twisted the arm till the man bent forward. He raised his knee into the attacker's face. The man sank to the floor like a sack of flour. The other two advanced cautiously as a pair. One was armed with a metal rod and the other had a cycle chain. Singh lifted a heavy wooden chair and threw it at them like it was a rubber ball. He charged in behind the flying furniture. He grabbed both the assailants by their necks; lifted them off the ground and threw them backwards. The rod wielder managed a lucky blow on the policeman's arm. Kamalbir merely winced, grabbed the man by the hair and slammed his head repeatedly into the wall. The rod crashed to the floor and so did the rod wielder. The one swinging cycle chain stood petrified on one spot. He threw the chain away as a gesture of capitulation; kneelt and started to cry. Singh judged him to be no more than eighteen years old. He slapped the lad hard across the face. The boy cowered in a corner, too frightened to move. 'Where is your boss?' Singh growled, between clenched teeth. The frightened lad did not answer. Singh slapped him again. 'He will return at any moment' the boy stuttered.

The don's heavy footsteps echoed in the narrow stairwell. The broken door and upset furniture stopped him in his stride. He figured that only constable Kamalbir would dare enter his lair. He regarded the intrusion as a direct challenge to his authority. The don believed he was invincible. He had dealt with the likes of Kamalbir before. He drew a nine inch blade from the scabbard and stepped inside the doorway. All his senses were alert to a surprise attack. The policeman was obviously nowhere in sight. Why don't you show yourself you damn coward?'

Singh had pressed his considerable bulk behind the sagging left door. He guessed the don was standing in the doorway. He slammed the door in the don's face and stepped into view. The don avoided the door and slashed the air with his knife. It ripped the front of the constable's shirt. Kamalbir swooped up a large wooden splinter and thrust it forward. The splinter pierced the don's arm. The don fought against the pain but his knife had slipped from his grasp. Singh leapt at his wounded adversary, slamming his shoulder into the don's chest. The don lurched backward, but recovered sufficiently to throw a punch at the policeman. The blow connected with Kamalbir's shoulder. The don was onto Singh in a flash. The two giants wrestled each other onto the wooden floor. They rolled from doorway and onto to the landing. Moments later the two adversaries rolled down the steep flight of stairs, locked in a deadly embrace. They ended on the pavement. The don pinned his opponent to the ground, lifted his right arm high and threw a punch at the policeman's bleeding face. Singh shifted his head and missed the crippling blow by a hair's breath. The don's fist hit the stone pavement. Kamalbir heard the sound of cracking knuckles. Singh managed a blow on the don's exposed throat. The don started to cough and wheeze. Singh threw the don off him and pounded his head repeatedly on the pavement. Singh placed his large knee on the don's throat and said between clenched teeth 'Nobody, but nobody threatens my family. If my child comes home with a mere scratch, I will track you down and kill you.' The victorious cop applied more pressure on the prostrate don's throat. 'You are under arrest for assaulting a policeman.' A throng of anxious onlookers, buoyed by the constable's victory, gathered the courage to applaud. They shouted hail Kamalbir like he had won a major war. The don faced a law suit that ended in a two years sentence and a fine of one thousand rupees.

CHAPTER 7

After a week Kamalbir returned for duty. He felt stiff and sore. He hoped the day would pass without incident. He ambled through the market place, exchanging pleasantries with the locals. A large expensive car turned into the lane. It was without doubt the car of a rich sahib. Sahibs were a rare sight in this part of town. If and when they did come, trouble was sure to follow. The car stopped at the entrance of the grocer's store. A young sahib stepped out of the car and entered the grocery. Kamalbir hoped to avoid the inevitable. He toyed with the idea of making himself scarce. But he knew that the recriminations would demand his presence. He decided to watch from a distance.

Kamalbir gaped in disbelief as the sahib and the local grocer hugged and back-slapped each other. This was a first. True the grocer was an amiable fellow, liked by all. But this went far beyond the boundaries of esteem and admiration. The event demanded urgent investigation. He paid the local moneylender a visit. The moneylender was the most reliable gossip monger of the neighbourhood. Singh's six feet four inches, two hundred pound frame filled the entrance of the moneylender's small office. The moneylender cold shouldered the policeman. The police had not heeded any of his complaints. His expression clearly indicated that Singh was not a welcome guest. Singh ignored the moneylender's unfriendly attitude and came directly down to business.

'What do you make of that?'

'Make of what?'

The love scene between the sahib and the grocer'

'It seems the grocer has a visitor. There is no need to consult Sherlock Holmes to deduce that.'

'I am not here for a lesson on detection. I want to know what's going on.'

'I just told you. The grocer has a visitor. It's a common occurrence. '

'And for you, this public display of love and friendship, between a sahib and a grocer is an everyday occurrence?'

'What would I know? I am a mere banker for whom the police have no regard.'

After much persuasion the moneylender opened up. 'Many years ago, when they were only children, the grocer saved the sahib's and his mother's life. In appreciation they bought him that shop. Every year his mother, the sahib's mother not the grocers, would return to India. She has never come here but she calls for him as soon as she lands in the city. Then she visits some village where all this is supposed to have happened. For some reason she has not visited India for years. This year the son has come instead of her. Maybe she is ill, too old to travel or even dead. I don't know.'

'What village? Where and when did this happen?'

'That is a closely guarded secret. Word has it that she had a temple constructed there. I am told it has brought her and the villagers nothing but happiness and good luck.'

'An English woman had a temple built in a village in the Bengal jungle? Are you bloody pulling my leg? Everyone from Calcutta to Cornwall would know about it.'

'I told you it was a closely guarded secret, pay attention.'

'And I suppose the woman in search of a confidant pulled your name out of a hat.'

'If you don't believe me, why don't you ask the grocer or the sahib?'

'I am in no mood for games.' Kamalbir's limited intelligence told him this was important news.

'Our wives are very close friends. That is the grocer's wife and mine, not yours or the sahib's. They tell each other everything.'

'It must be some temple, to make an old woman sail across the world, every year.'

'Not so much the temple. The statue that they installed in it is rumoured to be worth a number of manors and two estates in town. It is made of pure gold and studded with some of the finest diamonds, rubies and emeralds that money can buy.'

The constable needed to sit to digest the information. 'Thank you, I owe you one.'

'No, wait. I am not supposed to be aware of this. Neither the sahib's family nor the grocer ever speaks of this. It is information that is shared secretly by our wives. That is the grocer's wife and----'

'Yes, yes, I know which wives'

'If the grocer learns that his wife has opened her mouth, she will be in more trouble than Satan, if he strayed into heaven. For all his sterling qualities the grocer does have quite a temper.'

'Don't worry. Your secret is safe with me.'

The tale played on the constable's mind, all through the day. The event was scarcely believable. But the thought of a priceless artefact in the middle of nowhere demanded urgent investigation. He headed straight for the police station to share the information with his boss, friend and mentor, chief inspector Liam Crowe.

Liam Crowe was a master in executing underhanded shenanigans. He started life as a member of the London metropolitan police. He was the last of the Crowe family. They had loyally served the force for three generations. His uncle was the head detective at Scotland Yard. However, Liam was a blot on the good name of the Crowes. Rumours about his nephew's dubious dealings spread through the force. Torn between loyalty to the force and to his family's reputation, the uncle decided to place the matter before a panel of senior officials. To save the uncle any embarrassment they shipped Liam off to India. In India he started out as a junior inspector in the Bombay police force. He soon earned a reputation as a wily detective. Crime had reached epidemic proportions in Calcutta. Liam was transferred to the city as chief of the criminal investigation department. It was then that fate decided to bring him and Singh together. For about a year Crowe successfully solved a number of cases with Singh as his assistant. Criminals were arrested left, right and centre. Crowe and Singh formed a close friendship.

'The crow is cawing all day for you' a constable said as Singh entered the station. Singh found his boss pacing the floor and mumbling to himself. He turned and faced Singh with fire in his eyes. 'I am on the verge of solving the most complicated crime the Calcutta police have ever known. Everyone from the governor to the street vendor is closely watching my progress.

'This is the first I am hearing of this. Why is the street vendor privy to this information and not me?'

'How you came to be a policeman is a wonder'

Singh started to reveal his induction into the force, but Crowe stopped him. 'Just shut up and listen. Success in solving this crime would mean a promotion, a reward and accolades from London. But I have been taken off the case. Instead I have been relegated to the post of a nanny and chaperone, by order of the Viceroy himself. I am expected to hold the hand of a twenty four year old baby and escort him to a village, to meet the folk there. Good God man! What does the heir to one of the largest commercial empires in the world have in common with illiterate villagers? In all probability they can't even pronounce his name. The worst of it is that I have been left in the dark about a number of salient facts.' The words were like divine music to Kamalbir's ears. Everything the moneylender had said was true. 'At the end of the darkest tunnel there is light' Kamalbir said and waited for a reaction.

'Bear in mind that at the end of my foot there is a regulation sized shoe. Now stop drivelling and explain yourself.'

'God is showering his blessings on you. He works in mysterious ways his wonders to perform.'

'Are you drunk? By God, if you don't stop speaking in riddles I will perform a miracle that will leave you senseless.'

After years of association, Kamalbir knew when to quit. 'The moneylender told me there is a gold statue worth a fortune in that village. He learned of it from his wife, who in turn heard of it from the grocer's wife.'

'Do you hear what you are saying? A grocer's wife knows of a gold statue worth a fortune in a remote Indian village. The source of the information is the moneylender's wife. Since when have you been involved in women's baseless gossip? However, Singh's description of the statue made Crowe stop and think. 'Did she say how they came to possess it?' Don't tell me some heavenly soul presented them with it. Or did it just miraculously drop out of the sky?'

'As a matter of fact, some heavenly soul in the guise of an English woman did present them with it.'

'Really, an English woman spread out the map of India; closed her eyes and placed a finger on it. Her finger happened to fall on a remote village in Bengal. So she presented them with a priceless gold statue. She must have a lot of money and no brains.'

'She does have a lot of money. She is the mother of the heir to the Travers commercial empire.'

That information made Crowe stop and think. 'It still doesn't make sense. Those poor souls don't have a proper dish to cook and eat. They would slay one another for an ounce of silver, let alone a gold statue. And you want me to believe that they possess a priceless artefact?'

Singh shrugged his shoulders and said, 'I have told you what I know. The rest is up to you.'

Crowe mulled over the information. On the face of it, Singh's information made no sense. However, a multimillionaire was on his way to visit a remote village. The viceroy's involvement in the matter lent some credence to the story. He had no choice but to accept his new commission. A knot formed in the pit of Crowe's stomach. Wicked thoughts entered his head. The devil was raising his ugly head again. The "London days" were creeping up on him. The constable watched Crowe sit still and silent, tapping the desk top with his forefinger. He knew the devil was luring him into temptation. He left without excusing himself.

CHAPTER 8

Kamalbir awoke with a start to the sound of incessant knocking on his front door. He feared the don's men may have come to avenge their boss's incarceration. He peeped through a crack between the door and the jamb. The sight of Crowe surprised him. He gaped sleepily at the unexpected visitor. An ungainly bulge in his boxer shorts added to the comical aspect of the image. 'Tuck that thing away and get dressed very quickly. Pack a toothbrush. We may be away for a couple of days.' Crowe said with urgency in his voice.

A number of questions ran through Kamalbir's mind, but he dutifully obeyed. Crowe's little Morris chugged along, rolling and pitching over the bumpy road. 'Our first stop is St. Joseph's missionary hospital.'

'Why bother to travel a hundred miles, when there are a number of hospitals in town?'

'Are you always this irritating every morning?'

'Only when I am rudely awakened at the crack of dawn'

'Listen and do not speak. I want no opinions and no advice. We are going to investigate the truth behind the statue. Unless the higher authorities directly question you, please do not feel obliged to speak.'

'What exactly is this plan you have hatched?

'All will be revealed to you in good time.'

They arrived at the mission hospital around tea time. Reverend Beach who headed the mission, warmly welcomed the uninvited guests. Crowe informed the clergy of the purpose of his visit. Singh was served his afternoon tea in the pantry with the mission staff. He spent the night in their quarters. The disparity upset him. In his opinion it was a blatant act of social and ethnic discrimination.

At the stroke of dawn Crowe, Singh and Brother D'Cruz set off for the village in a bullock cart. Midway they encountered a range of hills. The tired oxen needed to be rested and watered after the strenuous uphill climb. The passengers enjoyed the panoramic view as they enjoyed breakfast. The cart driver made do with his humble homemade fare. The cart rolled into the village an hour after lunchtime. Brother D'Cruz introduced Crowe and Singh to the old priest. D'Cruz's presence assured the suspicious villagers of the stranger's credentials. The head priest flatly refused them entry into the Goddess's chamber.

Crowe surveyed the village with diligence that even impressed Singh. From the raised plinth of the temple he swept the open fields through his field glasses. He asked about a crumbling structure that stood roughly a mile from the village. He was told that it was an abandoned Hindu temple built more than three centuries ago. Crowe surveyed the area around the old abandoned temple. He earmarked it as the ideal place to hide. They were back at the hospital around dinner time. Reverend Beech forbade them to travel at night. He warned against wild animals and wilder humans. Crowe tried to allay the reverend's fears by reminding him that they were policemen. The reverend would have none of it. The following morning the Morris coughed and sputtered to life. Kamalbir was amused and a bit annoyed. He wondered aloud why Crowe insisted on travelling all this way to ask such senseless questions. Are there any other entrances to Travers' bedroom? How many entrances could there be to a room that could barely accommodate two cats. Will he be alone in the room? Did you expect a group of young belly dancing nuns to spend the night with him? Will anyone from the hospital, accompany him to the village? Yes, we are sending a French maid to bathe and dress him. With every question, Singh slapped his thigh and guffawed. 'Shut up you blasphemous wretch and let me think.' Crowe thought of a number of things that could go awry. From the priest's staunch refusal to show them the statue, he suspected it must be valuable.

Crowe sent in a preliminary report, convincing the governor to permit him and Singh to leave a day before Christopher's departure. He wished to ensure that no undesirable persons were anywhere near the village. He assembled a formidable police force to accompany Travers to the village. The governor arranged for a batch of military troupers to assist the police force. They were headed by major Carl Sanders. Crowe and Kamalbir left Calcutta at the first light of dawn. Singh snoozed as Crowe gunned the engine to try and reach the abandoned temple before sunset. About a mile from the hospital gate, Crowe drove the car off the road and onto the uneven terrain of a paddy field. Singh was nearly thrown off his seat. Through the mist of sleep he saw the car heading for a particularly large tree. He believed that Crowe had dozed and veered off the road. Singh screamed in fear. Crowe calmed his partner. He reminded Singh that they were headed for the derelict temple. He parked his car behind a cluster of tall bushes.

Weighed down by rations and other necessities, the two cops fought their way through the undergrowth. They panted and wheezed their way up the hill. Crowe scanned the expanse below him through his binoculars. In the distance the huts of the village looked like tiny brown polka dots on the barren earth. The dome of the temple shimmered in the midday sun, like a large gem set in a dust bowl. He focused his sights on the ancient ruin. It offered an unobstructed view of the temple. The thought that the villagers might spot them worried Kamalbir.

Crowe ignored his underling's paranoia. Crowe descended to the plains, slipping and stumbling all the way downhill. They approached the old temple ruins, travelling in a wide arc. Kamalbir was on tenterhooks. Singh's apprehension increased with every step. He stopped dead in his stride and warned 'I have given this matter close consideration. I am telling you here and now that I am not going anywhere near that temple. Whatever you plan to do, you will have to do it on your own.'

'What's the matter, I have never known you to have cold feet?'

'I have never in my life attempted to rob a temple. You have no idea of the consequences if we are caught? There is no law, no court, no police force and no head of state on earth that can save us from the wrath of these villagers. We will die a slow and painful death. Our only salvation will be God. And considering your past, I doubt if he will come to your rescue.'

'So you are planning to relax in the woods while I do all the dirty work?'

'No, I am planning to stay alive. My family means more to me than wealth.'

'Admit it, you are getting cold feet.'

'It is preferable to get cold feet than end up a cold carcass.'

CHAPTER 9

At dawn a convoy of cars and vans cruised through the empty streets of Calcutta. The scene was reminiscent of an Arab Sheik's caravan of camels. They were on their way to the missionary hospital. Major Sanders travelled with his charge in the Rolls Royce. He made Christopher sit in the middle of the rear seat, flanked by Walsh, Spratt and Bates. The farmlands and quaint villages disappeared. It seemed that civilisation had ceased to exist. The highway was hemmed in by thick forest on either side. Christopher decided to stop for brunch. It dismayed the colonel. He worried that they were exposed to a possible sneak attack. To add to his discomfort, a senior police officer warned that they were smack dab in the middle of dacoit country. The military and police surrounded the Rolls. Christopher, Spratt and Bates stepped out to stretch their legs. Walsh remained seated.

The beat of hooves and the tinkle of bells drifted towards them. A herd of domesticated cattle appeared from around a bend in the road. The herdsmen ran from one end to the other, trying to prevent the unruly cattle from straying. The chief police officer ordered the herdsmen to stop. The herdsmen obeyed, but the cattle refused to heed the officer. The distinct crack of a gunshot panicked the animals. The officer clutched his chest and fell where he stood. The entire force had their weapons aimed in the direction of the cattle. Dacoits appeared from within the herd and charged at the convoy. Colonel Harvey dragged Christopher into the car and shoved him onto the floorboard. He forbade him to raise his head. The charging dacoits were shredded by a barrage of the soldier's bullets. The surviving dacoits retreated into the relative safety of the woods. Man and beast lay on the road, wounded or dead. Another group of dacoits stormed the Rolls through the woods. The attack resulted in more deaths. The Rolls morphed into a fortified castle. Harvey borrowed a military assault rifle to defend the millionaire.

The dacoits descended on them from all four directions, firing indiscriminately. Walsh pressed himself against the floorboard next to Christopher. Spratt and Bates quickly crawled under the car. Harvey's assault rifle jammed when it was most needed. The dacoits reached the Rolls; wrenched open the rear door and grabbed Christopher by the collar. They attempted to pull him out. Walsh's massive bulk hampered their attempt to get a firm hold on Christopher. The millionaire clung to the seat with all his might. His grip slackened. He was dragged halfway out of the car. Harvey managed to reach the Rolls, firing his pistol at the abductors. A third dacoit attacked Harvey. The dacoit was no match for the S.A.S. officer. He slammed his head into the dacoit's jaw and followed with a volley of punches. More dacoits reached the car. Harvey shot two of the dacoits in the face at point blank range. A shower blood, flesh and bones rained down on the rear seat. With the swiftness of a striking cobra, Harvey grabbed the third dacoit's ear, pulled him close and pounded his face repeatedly until the man collapsed. A dacoit managed to seize Christopher. Christopher struggled to fight him off. From under the car Bates and Spratt grabbed the dacoit's legs and yanked them inward. The dacoit lost his balance and fell on his haunches like a toddler. The battle raged unabated. A dacoit crept in from behind the colonel Sanders, threw his arm round his neck and held him in a choke hold. Harvey grabbed the dacoit's head and face and broke his neck. The dacoit was dead before he fell to the ground. The surviving dacoits retreated into the woods and disappeared like phantoms. The unharmed soldiers and policemen began to take stock of the situation. A large number of policemen were wounded, some severely. A few were found dead. The military suffered just one fatal casualty.

Sanders opined that they were not dacoits. They were hired assassins out to kidnap Mister Travers. Dacoits don't single out a victim he explained. They are not interested in individuals; they are interested in their cash and valuables. The dacoits were paid to divert our attention.

The convoy arrived at the mission hospital well after dinnertime. A group of anxious priests waited at the gate to welcome the guest of honour. Reverend Beech, who headed the reception committee, was riddled with anxiety.

CHAPTER 10

The following day, Christopher and company made their way to the village. Soon the carts entered the forest. The uneven terrain made the passengers rock and sway like drunken sailors. A thick canopy of leaves spread like a large green umbrella above them. The undergrowth spread out like a matching carpet. The morning dew lent a shimmering lustre to the foliage. By midday they braved the steep narrow climbs, sheer edges, and sharp curves. They reached the top without incident. While the animals rested, Christopher and company admired the artistic prowess of mother-nature. The drivers deftly guided the animals down the steep slope and onto the barren plains. The summer sun had baked the earth dry. They reached the village late afternoon.

The sights, sounds and smells rolled back the years, leaving Christopher in a reminiscent trance. He was adorned with a colourful garland of wild flowers and anointed with saffron coloured religious symbols. He headed straight for the old priest's hut as soon as the welcome ritual ended. A bamboo fence cordoned off the hut. Christopher laid a bunch of flowers at the entrance. Reverend Beech was also received as an honoured guest. He held a special place in the hearts of the villagers. Harvey, Sanders, Walsh, Spratt, and Bates were received cordially. Christopher noticed a marked change in the village and the villagers. The men and women looked healthy and well clad. The undernourished children were now robust little brats. The old thatched huts were gone. The new dwellings were small, but made of bricks and mortar. Only the old priest's hut remained untouched. The fields on the outskirts of the village were lush green. The paddy fields boasted of a promising harvest. Walsh, Spratt and Bates bided their time eyeing the ladies.

As the sun dipped behind the hills, the villagers gathered at the temple for evening prayers. However the number of attendees was far smaller than before. Later they all retreated into the sanctuary of their homes. The village square and the single road lay deserted. One by one the windows and doors darkened. Christopher lay on his charpoy remembering the old days. The stress of the trip soon caught up with him. He drifted off into a deep slumber. At the first glow of dawn, two apprentice priests entered Christopher's hut. They immersed his naked body into an icy cold stream. Christopher let out a cry that awoke the entire village. They draped Christopher in a saffron coloured shawl and carried him to the temple. It was now time for him to be spiritually cleansed. The sun peeped over the horizon, spreading a dim glow on the village and the plains. Soon the entire village came alive with vibrant enthusiasm. Men and women fussed over their allocated chores. Children ran around in a frenzy of joyous senselessness, annoying everyone. The preparations for the ritual kept everyone on their toes.

****

Singh, who had spent a restless night, awoke with a start. He thought he heard the faint wail of a tortured soul in the distance. He tried to see through grey haze of dawn with Crowe's binoculars. A blank sheet of grey pressed against the lens. He guessed that the rituals would soon commence. Hesitantly he shook his snoring partner awake. Crowe was vexed by the lack of Singh's concern. 'Are you, a lark? It's barely dawn.'

Crowe trained his binoculars on the village square. He too could see nothing. But he heard the faint sounds of activity. They poured tepid tea out of a flask and waited for things to get a little brighter. Crowe trained his binoculars on the temple. He could now see silhouettes of the villagers busy with their chores. The sound of their chanting reached the ruin. 'Tomorrow morning we too will be singing with joy' he mumbled with a smile.

'There is a chance, you may be singing with Angels.'

'Oh stop your pessimistic moaning. I am going to make us both rich. You and all your descendants will praise and thank me. They will kneel and pay homage to a large portrait of me hanging in their living rooms. They will sing songs of praise and gratitude to their uncle Liam.'

'It is far more likely you will be hanging from the limb of a tree. The villagers will shout curses at you.'

'Now let's make our way to the village. We must make our presence known to the millionaire and convince him of our diligence.'

The countryside terrain tested Crowe to the full. He tripped over stones, stumbled into potholes and fell on his haunches more than once. Crowe reported his presence to the colonel. He pointedly ignored everyone else. The head priest announced that Christopher would not be permitted to socialise until after the ritual. The announcement baffled Crowe. He believed this was a joyous occasion. Harvey gave Crowe a piece of his mind for his absence during the dacoit raid. A heated argument ensued. The confrontation threatened to turn violent. Crowe turned on his heels and left the temple in a huff. Singh silently followed his boss.

CHAPTER 11

Christopher's cleansing ceremony was about to commence. Dark heavily laden rainclouds rolled in and hung over the festivities. It troubled the head priest. Rain was a portent of disaster on an auspicious occasion. He was tempted to postpone the celebrations. But then again, there was no guarantee what tomorrow would bring. He was taught that the fate of every living being was preordained. He decided to risk it.

Holy water was sprinkled over Christopher. He was escorted into the Goddess's sanctum and stripped to the waist. They sat him down cross legged on a carpet of petals and leaves in front of the Goddess's niche. Soon the head priest started to recite verses from the Gita. The sound of chanting and the tolling of bells carried onto the congregation hall. The chanting created a soothing hypnotic effect on the minds and souls of all those present. Pin drop silence fell on the congregation hall. Walsh and his cronies stood by the entrance of the inner chamber. The thought of Christopher adorned with red and yellow symbols conjured up the picture of a Red Indian Chief. The vision made Walsh chuckle. It drew threatening glares from the reverend and Harvey. The ceremony ended in a crescendo of chanting, accompanied by peels of the large and small bells. Christopher was made to lie on his stomach before the Goddess with his hands joined above his head. The head priest held a hand over Christopher's head and recited a short prayer. Christopher was told to silently make a wish. Thereafter, the guests were permitted to enter the inner chamber. Reverend Beech was followed by Harvey, Spratt, Bates and lastly Walsh. The villagers were the last to enter.

The head priest blessed each passing guest. The junior priests poured a teaspoonful of sanctified sweet milk in their cupped palms. Walsh stood transfixed in front of the niche with his eyes riveted on the statue. Evil thoughts possessed him. He was prepared to sell his soul to the devil to get his hands on it. Those behind him grew impatient. The head priest read Robert's mind. Robert was forced to move on without milk or blessing.

Apart from the weather, the presence of Walsh continued to trouble the head priest. He was convinced of an impending disaster. He tried his best to delay Christopher's departure. Christopher responded with scientific arguments. The priest finally left Christopher's fate in the hands of God.

The cart carrying Christopher and his colleagues left well after the others were gone. They were accompanied by two armed soldiers. Dark clouds persistently hovered overhead. The head priest, his wife and son started for the temple. All his wife's attempts to raise her husband's sprits failed miserably. The evil guest continued to haunt his thoughts. The sombre tones of twilight painted the sky. He started to prepare for the evening prayers.

CHAPTER 12

The deep resonance of the big bell carried all the way to the ruin. Singh knew it heralded the start of the evening prayers. A knot of fear formed in the pit of his stomach. He sat silently contemplating his plight. Crowe, oblivious of the consequences was bent on purloining the statue. Singh planed ways to wriggle out of the affair. A plethora of excuses to avoid entering the temple ran through his mind. But leaving Crowe to bell the cat could prove suicidal. The man would not hesitate to throw him to the wolves. The wily wolf would find a way to save his skin. He resigned himself to the fact that this is where he would die. It was not the where but the how that petrified him.

Singh watched Crowe, snoring under a spreading tree with his mouth open. The sight awoke the childish prankster in him. Singh placed a bug on Crowe's nose. Crowe jolted out of his slumber and repeatedly slapped his face. He looked about him, dazed and disoriented. Singh's guffawing annoyed him. He fixed a menacing glare on his subordinate. 'Are you a bloody adolescent? Have you no consideration for others? I have spent the better part of the day traversing up and down a natural obstacle course. The sun, having nothing better to do, decided to try and roast me alive, and believe me he damn nearly succeeded. I was compelled to cross swords with that military muttonhead, Colonel Hardy or Hartley or whatever his name is. I was forced to endure the cacophony of what those peasants refer to as music. I mingled with the guests and villagers, wearing a fixed smile like a mongoloid child. Since our return, I have tried to get some rest. But pebbles, stones and other sharp objects decided to gang up against me. No matter where I turned, they sharpened themselves and crept under me. Every insect in the neighbourhood felt socially obligated to pay me a visit. They crawled all over my arms and face. The tree, bored by years of standing still, decided to rain leaves and twigs on me. And when I finally fell asleep, you decided to play your childish prank. We will approach the temple at midnight and no sooner. Till then, kindly amuse yourself in any way you deem fit.' Having had his say, Crowe returned to his slumber. Moments later the sound of his snoring filled the air.

Singh sat ill at ease, fearing the approach of villagers. He decided that if he sighted one, he would flee, leaving his snoring partner to his own fate. The night had pushed away the last vestiges of dusk. Her black cloak covered everything. Singh feared villagers more than predators. However he nearly jumped out of his skim when a cat roared close by. Late evening Crowe stretched and yawned. He called out to Singh in a stage whisper. There was no reply. Crowe feared the constable had lost his nerves and fled. The shrill songs of the creepy crawly denizens started to get on his nerves. He damned Travers' mother for her generosity and kindness. He damned Singh for having introduced him to this infernal scheme and damned himself for his greed. After what seemed hours, Singh appeared from behind a bush, adjusting his trousers.

CHAPTER 13

By mid-afternoon Christopher's cart reached the top of the hill. A blanket of fog kept visibility to a minimum. A light passing shower had made the path difficult to manoeuvre. The cart driver was apprehensive. With a prayer on his lips, he urged his oxen forward. The passengers remained tense and apprehensive. The oxen descended painfully slowly for about quarter of the way downhill. A hundred yards before them lay the hairpin bend that every cart driver dreaded. The width of the bend was barely wider than the cart. The handler expertly guided the animals. A bush rustled in the immediate vicinity. The booming roar of a large cat spooked the oxen. They stomped their hooves, bucked and reared in an effort to get away. They darted forward in a state of blind panic. Well into the hairpin bend, the outer wheel slid towards the edge. It created a minor landslide. The wheel of the cart slipped off the edge, throwing cart, beasts and men over the cliff. The sound of splintering wood and screams of panic reverberated as the cart tumbled into the abyss. The heavens announced the tragedy with a clap of thunder and a bolt of lightning. The wind howled mournfully over the tragedy. The denizens of the forest continued with their daily business, unconcerned.

Robert Walsh opened his eyes and gazed blankly at the dark grey clouds. Gradually his brain cells started to tick. The entire incident came to him in fits and starts. Walsh heaved himself up and felt his limbs and torso for fractures. He was surprised that he had come away with only minor injuries. His eyes swept the hilltop in the hope of finding another survivor. The thought of being alone among predators and phantoms filled him with dread. He contemplated on his situation. To head for the hospital was the sensible thing to do. He knew that he was far from the missionary hospital. But he would be forced to trudge through miles of thick jungle. By then the sun would have retired. The fear of getting lost or being devoured by wild animals urged him to reconsider. The way to the village was over flat open shrub land. If he hurried, he could reach it before sunset. The thought of the village brought to mind the image of the statue. It would remain unguarded till dawn. The temptation to steal it was overwhelming. He planned several strategies and pondered over the risks. The adage nothing ventured, nothing gained urged him on. It suddenly occurred to him that he was in a unique situation. The whole world believed he was lying dead in the valley. It gave him the freedom to do as he pleased.

He turned to head for the village. Movement at the edge of the cliff arrested his attention. A soft guttural voice called out his name. His heart skipped a beat. A maimed and bloodied body was calling out for help. Walsh walked over and recognised Spratt. A look of hope washed over Spratt's face. For one brief moment Walsh was torn between compassion and wealth. He kicked Spratt under the chin. The unfortunate man flew backwards; his arms flayed helplessly in the air as he disappeared over the edge of the cliff. Walsh turned and started to trudge downhill. He reached the barren plains below and walked purposefully towards his tryst with fate.

CHAPTER 14

Around midnight, Crowe awoke and searched for Singh. Crowe started to worry. He feared that the constable might have lost his nerve and fled. Crowe swore he would spend the rest of his life tracking him down. And when he did, the spineless rat would beg for death. Singh sensed Crowe's agitation. He grabbed Crowe's shoulder and speaking in Hindi, he said the Sikh man told us that you are here to steal our statue. Crowe froze with fear. Singh would have continued with the prank had he not started to titter. Crowe punched Singh in his chest and called him all sorts of names. The peels of temple bells marked the end of Singh's tomfoolery.

Crowe was not accustomed to activity in rural surroundings. The sheer darkness made matters worse. 'It worried him. 'How do you suggest we negotiate the natural obstacle course? 'You tell me. You are the boss; this is your project, so you lead the way.' Crowe overlooked Singh's insubordination. Right now, he needed the dim witted giant more than ever. Crowe suggested the use of quick bursts of the torch to guide them.

'Not even the village idiot will mistake a torch for a firefly. Fireflies are tiny insects. Your torch reflector is the size of a cricket ball. These village folk know their rural surroundings as well as we know the city. They can differentiate a tiger from a leopard just from the shine of its eyes.' Singh responded angrily. He advised they move one careful step at a time and hope for the best.

'You lead the way' Crowe insisted, reminding Singh of his rural background.

'You are the boss. It is my duty to follow you.'

'If the circumstances were different, I would gladly punch you in the face.'

'If the circumstances were different, I would not be here.'

They agreed to walk shoulder to shoulder. Singh heard Crowe utter a string of profanities under his breath every time he slipped and stumbled. There was panic and irritation in his voice. Suddenly Singh heard something thrash about in a bush. He tried to identify the source.

'Don't just stand there like a totem pole, come here and help me. I think I have walked into some unearthly creature. It has taken a firm hold of me.'

'How do you mean you think? Either something has got hold of you or it has not. Even a man with limited intelligence would know that.'

Crowe continued to kick and thrash, spewing expletives at his partner.

Singh reached for his boss's tweed jacket and extricated it from a thorny bush.

'As if I didn't know that it was a bush' Crowe said sheepishly.

They continued at the pace of tortoises on a leisurely stroll. Crowe asked Singh to estimate the distance to the temple. 'It could be a mile, it could be a hundred. How would I know?' Singh heard his boss call out to him. It seemed to emit from the bowels of the earth. Singh took an irritatingly long time to locate Crowe. As soon as Crowe was out he gave Singh a piece of his mind. A hundred yards later he tripped over a stone and fell face down in a pool of wet mud. Garbled sounds like the gurgle of bathwater seeping through a drain emitted from the ground. He walked back towards the inexplicable sounds. To his surprise a dark blob on the ground moved, rose and stood facing him. Singh gaped at Crowe bewildered. Crowe yanked the water flask from Singh's shoulder and gargled and washed his face.

Crowe's ordeal was over once they arrived at the temple. It stood tall and majestic in the darkness. To Singh it looked like some prehistoric creature, waiting to swallow him. The village was seeped in deathly silence. Singh crouched behind a hedge and refused to go any further. Crowe volunteered to survey the area. He ordered Singh to warn him of any approaching villager. Singh asked if he should shout beware villager or send him a telepathic message.

Crowe leapfrogged onto the open congregation hall and crept towards the inner chamber. To his surprise, he found the door ajar. The dancing oil lamps threw intermediate glows at the base of the door. He strained his ears for tell-tale sounds. All was still and silent. Summoning his courage, he stepped into the chamber. An involuntary gasp escaped his lips. He stood motionless, trying to make sense of the grizzly sight before him. Crowe called out for Singh. The call sent a chill down Singh's spine. His hair stood on end like a porcupine's quills. He wondered if it was a cry for help or fear. Singh's first instinct was to flee. He decided to wait and see how events unfolded. At the end of many tense moments Crowe appeared beside him. It caused Singh to jump and squeal, like a spooked squirrel. Crowe's demeanour convinced Singh that something was very wrong. He warily followed Crowe through the door of the inner chamber. He was confronted by a scene that froze every sinew in his body. An assortment of religious items littered the floor. Rivulets of burning oil and blood meandered across the room. In the middle of the chamber the head priest lay in a pool of blood. The long handle of a trident protruded out of his chest like some heavenly antenna. Crowe squatted and checked the body for signs of life. The warmth of the carcass told him that death was fairly recent. Singh threw a quick glance over the outer area of the temple. A sack of sorts lay draped over the edge of the congregation hall. He stared at it fixedly. It did not move. Crowe checked out the niche that housed the statue. To his horror and utter disappointment it lay empty. The sound of an angry mob rushing towards the temple drifted over the still night air. The two policemen leapt into the darkness and fled into the relative safety of the wilderness like two startled gazelles.

CHAPTER 15

After a moment of family fun in the temple, the priest commenced preparations for the evening prayers. An owl hooted in the neighbouring tree. A jackal bayed in the distance. A field mouse dropped in uninvited for a bit of potluck. The son threw him a small piece of chapatti. The crickets and grasshoppers sang out their love songs. Everything seemed normal. The priest left his wife and son to attend to his religious duties. A faint scraping sound in the outer hall arrested the priest's attention. He recognised they were not the footsteps of herbivores. Carnivores would make no sound at all. The memory of the evil guest entered his mind. Since he was a slip of a boy, he was trained in the art of single combat. He removed a trident from the wall and kept it close at hand. The flickering flames threw light in one part of the chamber and then another. Half a face appeared from behind the doorway. Gradually more of the man came into view. The priest grabbed the trident and stepped into the darkness. There by the doorway stood the priest's greatest fear. When the evil intruder was within striking distance, the priest lunged at the villain. The villain stepped back with surprising agility, avoiding the prongs by a hair's breadth. The priest lunged forward again. The evil guest lifted his leg and reached for his boot. Taking advantage of the moment, the priest managed a lucky blow. Blood oozed from the cut on the intruder's chest. The two adversaries circled one another in the confined space. The intruder sliced the air with his knife in an attempt to confuse the priest. Each time the priest stepped back to avoid the knife, the intruder inched closer. With his back to the wall, the priest had no option but to attack. He thrust the trisul forward in desperation, inflicting another bloody wound. Pressing the advantage, the priest attempted a full on attack. The villain grabbed the trisul just under the prongs and yanked at it with all his strength. The priest lurched forward, losing his grip on his sacred weapon. The villain inflicted a deep wound on the priest's face. The villain seemed unsure of his next move. Taking advantage of the hesitation, the priest sprang like a leopard, slamming his shoulder into the villain's chest. The villain staggered backward into a shelf. A variety of religious items came raining down on the marble floor, in a deafening crescendo. The intruder lost his knife in the scuffle. The priest was upon him in a flash, pinning his opponent against the wall and digging his elbow into the throat. The intruder grabbed the priest's genitals and squeezed with all his might. He pushed the priest's head back and broke his nose with his head. The priest staggered and fell on his back like a felled tree. The villain swept up the trident and plunged it into the priest's chest. He stood over the dead priest, breathing heavily.

Walsh retrieved his knife and waited to catch his breath. A high pitched piercing cry caused him to start and turn. A woman charged at him out of the darkness, screeching like a creature from hell. Her eyes flashed with unbridled fury. She held her hands in front of her like the claws of a cat. Her teeth were bared in a horrifying grimace. The woman clawed and kicked wildly at Walsh's face and body. Walsh pushed her back with all his strength. The woman stumbled backward and very nearly fell. She realised she was no match for the evil monster. She needed reach the village for help. She turned and ran out of the chamber and into the open congregation hall. Walsh could not afford any eyewitnesses. He caught up with her just as she was about to leap off the congregation hall. He grabbed her by the hair, pulled her towards him and thrust his knife into her back. She arched backward and collapsed in a heap. Half her lifeless body lay draped over the edge of the hall. He wiped his blood drenched knife with her sari and returned to the chamber.

The priest's six years old son sat huddled in the darkest corner of the storeroom. He saw the villain enter holding an oil lamp. It stopped in the doorway and looked about him. The child followed the intruder's movements with his eyes. It looked like some satanic fiend from hell. It started its search at the other end. It lifted an assortment of items; examined them and threw them aside with a disappointed grunt. Gradually it worked his way towards the child. The child remained in a foetal position, petrified with mind numbing fear. His eyes remained fixed on his would be killer. The monster stood next to some crates and looked around the room. His giant sized boots were only inches away. The child held his breath, hoping the Goddess would come to his aid. The sickening stench of the man's sweat filled the room. Just when the child expected to be caught and devoured by the fiend, it lifted an empty gunny bag with a sigh of satisfaction and stepped out of the storeroom. The child decided to flee. He crept to the storeroom door and peered from behind the doorjamb. The monster had its back to him. The demon was busy wrapping the statue in the gunnysack. Mustering all his courage, he darted out like a scalded cat, leapt off the side and fled toward the village.

Walsh heard the patter of feet and spun round. The still and silent Goddess's chamber stared back at him. He put it down to his imagination. He wrapped the statue in the gunnysack, tied it with the priest's scarf, slung the heavy load over his shoulder and walked out into the night. Walsh left the temple believing this to be the beginning of a journey to millions.

The trudge to the hills left him exhausted. It appeared forbiddingly high in the darkness. The weight of the statue proved more cumbersome than he anticipated. He willed himself to continue uphill. Every ten minutes he needed to stop and transfer the sack to the other shoulder. Halfway to the peak, his body threatened to fall apart. He lost the will to continue. At the inner end of the footpath, the hillside rose at a fairly steep angle. It was covered by a cluster of tall bushes. He took refuge behind one of them and drifted into a deep slumber.

Walsh awoke with a start. He looked about him disoriented. The gentle breeze had strengthened, blowing dust and debris every which way. The wind wailed like a weeping woman. The mournful sound grew louder with every passing moment. He noticed a whirlwind rise up from the valley below. The swirling column of air appeared to resemble a slender woman pirouetting towards him. The hum grew louder, the apparition grew taller, and the wind hit gale force strength. The pirouetting ballerina passed within a few feet of him. She appeared to be looking his way. Her eyes burned through him like laser beams. The sound was deafening. An eerie chill passed through him. The apparition faded away. The wind and the hum died as quickly as it started. The still silence of wildernesses returned to envelope the hill. He thought he had gone deaf. It worried him. All of a sudden, the squeaks and chirrups of nocturnal forest creatures filled the air. It sounded like arias from a Verdi opera. He almost sang out one in joyous celebration.

Walsh mulled over the eerie experience. He believed he had experienced some supernatural phenomena. An unshakable fear possessed him. Had he provoked the wrath of divine powers? Before the temple incident, he would have rubbished the thought. Now he was in two minds. He had heard a number of stories of people in India regularly experiencing similar events. A few had sworn by it. The possibility that he had provoked a divine entity, sent chills down his spine. It was rumoured that those who angered the divine suffered from debilitating diseases, crippling accidents and even permanent insanity. The still silence of the wilderness was pierced by a loud shriek. It was soon followed by another. He wondered if the spirits of his victims were coming to get him.

CHAPTER 16

Crowe blundered his way uphill. He lit his torch to get his bearings. Singh turned on his boss with ire fuelled by fear and incredulity. After a heated argument, Crowe reluctantly switched off his torch. Halfway up Crowe could barely take another step. His chest felt like it was being squeezed in a vice grip. His lungs threatened to explode. His legs felt like they were about to fall off. Wheezing and panting, he gestured to Singh to stop. The two partners in crime sat beside a tall bush. Crowe let out a loud sigh of relief. The peak appeared to be touching the clouds. A bleak grey sky hung overhead. Crowe suddenly shrieked, jumped up and broke into an epileptic dance. Singh looked on in utter bewilderment. Crowe's comical antics were intruded upon by an eerie hum. It grew louder as the wind intensified in strength. They gaped goggle-eyed as the whirlwind emerged from the valley and onto the hillside. Singh followed its progress like a man hypnotised. The powerful whirlwind sped past them and vanished as quickly as it started. Crowe paid little heed to it. Singh said that the Goddess just passed by. Crowe eyed his compatriot, amused. He asked if she was out on her daily constitutional and guffawed. To enlighten his junior, he explained that it was only a natural occurrence called whirlwinds. Singh remained unconvinced. He pointed out that not a leaf had fluttered and not an ounce of dirt had been disturbed. He added that in India the divine rules supreme. There are no scientific explanations for such occurrences. Crowe remained unconvinced.

****

Walsh was shaken by Crowe's inhuman screech. He decided it was best to stay well away. In his haste to get away, he lost his footing and fell. A large chunk of loose soil and stones rolled downhill onto the path below. 'Look, the Goddess is pelting us with stones' he heard someone say between peals of laughter. Walsh waited with bated breath for a reaction. The pair remained where they were. Walsh hurried away from the spot. He was eager to get to the mission hospital. He arrived at the fatal bend. The accident ran through his mind with chilling clarity. He noticed hooves, bones and a myriad of personal items littering the path. He felt depressed. But this was not the time for sentimental retrospection. He did not linger. He reached the woods later than he hoped. The sun hung low in the western sky. But he was a spent force. He did not have the strength, the energy or the will to move another step. The woods provided ample places to remain unseen. There was always a chance he might be spotted by some passing woodsman. But then, woodsmen did not pose a threat. Walsh found a spot that gave him adequate cover from any approaching passerby. He made a makeshift pillow from fallen leaves and almost immediately sank into the dreamless. He was awoken by an overfriendly beetle. He brushed it off his face; slung the sack over his shoulder and continued his trek.

****

Crowe and Singh clambered to the top of the hill puffing, panting and sweating. Crowe descended the hillside like a disjointed toy. The slippery earth and lose gravel tested him to the full. After a number of minor mishaps they approached the fatal bend. The sight made them stop in their strides. It was evident there had been a tragic mishap. He expertly inspected the scene. A broken cart wheel was evidence that a villager had miscalculated the bend. Singh pointed out the expensive items strewn across the path. It sent a tremor down their spines. They looked at one another, unwilling to voice what they secretly feared. They spent nearly an hour at the accident site. Singh observed that the accident could not have occurred too long ago. Passing forest dwellers would have taken the objects long before now. The two cops continued their trek in silence. Finally Crowe voiced his concern. 'If that was Travers's cart we had best avoid the hospital' he advised. Singh was too busy thinking of places where he and his family might escape from the law.

****

The sun had risen over the eastern horizon. Walsh guessed it would soon be breakfast time at the missionary hospital. The thought of breakfast started his gastric juices flowing. Hunger burned the pit of his stomach. The vision of fried eggs, freshly baked bread, hot tea and fruits floated before him. He dismissed the image from his mind. The dull glow of dawn made travel easier. He forced his legs to take one painful step at a time. Finally the roof of the hospital peeped over the trees. He feared a passing priest might recognise him. It was imperative that he clear out of the area in a hurry. The problem of reaching Calcutta confronted him. He decided to deal with one problem at a time. He cut a path parallel to the mission road. He was wary and alert. A shimmering reflection arrested his attention. It appeared to be something that did not belong to the rural surroundings. He warily approached the strange object. He could barely believe his eyes. A shiny black Morris waited patiently among the bushes. It was a baffling conundrum. People don't leave cars in forested areas without a reason. He pondered over it. He believed in not looking a gift horse in the mouth. With his knife he ripped open the soft top and folded it back. He found the crank handle under the front passenger seat. On the fifth crank the engine coughed and sputtered to life. Walsh was ecstatic. He drove away.

Hunger pangs gnawed at his stomach walls. He called on all his willpower to concentrate on driving the car. An hour later, Walsh arrived at a hamlet. He spotted a fruit vendor standing behind his handcart. He reached for his wallet in his hip pocket. It wasn't there. His hunger and fatigue vanished. In panic and desperation he searched all the pockets repeatedly. He stopped the car on the side of the road and carefully inspected every nook and cranny of the vehicle. The fact that his he was penniless hit him hard. But he had experienced such situations before. He waited for the vendor's customers to leave. Then he eased the car slowly and silently alongside the cart, grabbed a bunch of bananas and sped away. He wolfed down six before his hunger pangs started to ease.

Walsh steered the little Morris into Calcutta city limits at the speed of an unhurried turtle. Speeding cars often attract the wrong kind of attention. The lengthening shadows of dusk crept over the city. Everything around him looked unfamiliar. This was not the part of Calcutta to which Travers had introduced him. His first priority was to get rid of the car. It had a Calcutta registration number. There was the possibility that the owner could be residing only a street away. He turned off the main road into a deserted lane. A row of warehouses lined one side of the street. All of them had downed their shutters. A column of Lorries lined the other side. There were no warehouse personnel or lorry drivers around. He parted with his four-wheeled saviour with a heavy heart, leaving the key in it. Hopefully the key might tempt a dishonest passer-by. Hopefully the passer-by would be caught. Walsh looked up and down the deserted lane several times, fearful that some good for nothing fellow might be watching him. Not even a stray dog was in sight. The warehouses and trucks were indications of an industrial neighbourhood. He figured the docks and railway station should be within close proximity. Considering the circumstances, it was best he flee the city as quickly as possible. For that he needed money. It did not matter if he begged, borrowed or stole. The last was the most feasible option.

****

Singh arrived where the Morris had been parked a few minutes after Crowe. He had stopped to relieve himself. He found Crowe running around the bushes in circles, cursing like a drunken sailor. It took Singh a moment to realise that the car was missing. Crowe behaved like an overwrought woman who had lost her child. He cursed Christopher, he cursed the viceroy, he cursed the chief of police, he cursed the missionary priests and he cursed his stupidity for getting involved in the affair. Singh leant against a tree calmly watching his boss's antics. He knew that even a sympathetic word would make the Irishman fly off the handle. Singh finally advised Crowe to calm down and think.

'Stop telling me to calm down' Crowe replied between clenched teeth. 'My car is stolen. I am nearly two hundred miles from home. I am in a place, at a time, where and when I have no business to be. So when the chief starts asking questions, kindly answer calmly for me.'

"We don't know it was stolen. Maybe---"

'They will want positives answers, not maybes. Maybe can be anything. Maybe it got bored and went for a stroll. Maybe it sprouted wings and flew away. I can think of a million maybes, but I cannot think of a single rational explanation. The fact is that it was definitely stolen.'

'I was going to say, maybe a priest found it and had it pushed to the missionary home.'

The suggestion sent a chill down Crowe's spine. 'That would be the final nail in my coffin' he stuttered.

'I don't understand.'

'Do you ever? How am I going to explain myself? Stop staring at me like a befuddled baboon. Why did I park my car here, when the missionary compound is only a mile away? Where was I at the time of Travers' departure from the village? What could have kept me there for so long? Why did I not travel with my charge? Now do you understand?' Crowe said agitatedly. Crowe's brain worked overtime, searching for answers to a million questions he knew the authorities would throw at him.

'Let's take a peep in the compound. If it is there we'll cook up some plausible story.' Singh waited warily for another round of hysteria.

'You want to risk a peek, go ahead and do so? I will remain here. If you are caught, don't expect any help from me. Before you embark on your adventure, explain how you plan to go about this reconnaissance mission? Do you plan to drill a hole in that solid teak gate? Knock on the gate and ask whoever answers if they found a car parked in the middle of nowhere. Fashion a makeshift periscope. And how will you explain yourself if you are recognised?

Finally Crowe conceded that Singh's suggestion was worth a shot. He watched the constable scramble up the ten feet high compound wall and peer over. The branches of a large tree hindered Singh's view of the garage. He recognised the reverend's Austin van, a cycle and a couple of wheel barrows, but no Morris. A loud voice in a heavy Scottish accent directly below him caused Singh to start, lose his footing and come crashing down at the feet of reverend Beech. The embarrassed and flustered constable stood up as fast as he could to face the stern looking priest.

'Well?'

'Yes. Thank you.'

'I am not interested in your state of health. I wish to know why you were perched on my wall like a monkey.'

'Someone stole our car.'

'And you suspect us?'

'No, no'

'Then why were you peering over the mission wall?'

'I thought maybe someone had found it and brought it here.'

'Then why did you not come in and ask?'

'Ask what?'

'Ask about the car.'

'I know about the car. It was stolen.'

'Where was the car before you lost it?'

'It was a mile down the road.'

'And where were you?'

'Where was I, when?'

'Where were you when the car was stolen?'

'I don't know when the car was stolen.'

'God Almighty' the reverend sighed. 'What have I done to deserve this?'

He took a deep breath. 'Why did you leave your car and go wherever you went?'

'It is not my car it belongs to my senior officer. He left it there because he was on an urgent secret official business.'

'Regarding Mister Travers, am I correct?'

'Yes'

'Are you in charge?'

'No sir. Chief Inspector Crowe is in charge.'

'And where is this chief inspector Crowe?'

'He is right there' Singh replied, pointing to empty space behind him. He turned to see an empty road looking back at him. 'He was here only moments ago' Singh replied sheepishly.

'You seem to have lost him too.'

Singh and the reverend looked up and down the empty road, bemused and peeved.

'Tell the chief inspector I wish to speak to him urgently, if you can find him.'

Moments after the reverend left the scene, Crowe appeared on the scene like a phantom. He noticed the rage on his partner's face and started to explain. 'I saw someone approaching, so I hid behind the bush. I hoped he would not notice you on the wall. But I should have known that not even the blind could miss a gorilla on a wall. However, I must salute you. For the first time, your inadequacy of the English language and lack of intelligence has proved to be useful.'

'Whatever, the reverend wants to have a word with you.'

Reverend Beech sat behind his desk, his countenance grim and austere. 'Before we start I strictly prohibit this man from uttering a single word at any time and for any reason' he said, pointing to Singh. 'He seems to have acquired the annoying ability to turn a simple conversation into a Vaudeville cross talk.'

When he faced Crowe, his controlled anger was plainly visible.

'I believe you were given the responsibility for the wellbeing of Mister Travers.'

'Yes father'

'For the love of God I don't see why. Of all the capable officers in His Majesty's service what possessed them to pick you?'

'I resent that father. I have done everything humanly possible to ensure Travers' safety.'

The reverend stared at Crowe, his hands trembling with rage. He came within an ace of throwing a brass paper weight at the inspector. 'Is that so? You seem to be oblivious of the events that occurred since Travers left the village. Are you aware that five people lie dead in the valley? Are you aware that the man you were supposed to protect narrowly escaped death? The infinite mercy of the Lord spared us the pain. He sent a dedicated and resourceful army officer in the nick of time to rescue Mister Travers.'

'By army officer, you don't mean that imperious idiot?'

The reverend ignored the comment. 'When the cart rolled over, Colonel Harvey fell on the stump of a dead tree, sticking out of the hillside. He noticed someone lying on a narrow ledge fifteen feet below. He recognised Mister Travers. With creditable skill and agility he managed to reach Mister Travers. All his efforts to get Travers to stand failed. The colonel threw Travers over his shoulder and lugged him all the way here. While all this was going on, what were you doing? You were bungling around in the forest, losing automobiles and scaling walls. It is a shameful state of affairs.'

'Where is Travers?'

'He is in capable hands. Now please leave.'

After a lot of coaxing and pleading, the reverend agreed to have a mission priest drive the two policemen to Calcutta in the van.

****

Walsh walked out of the lane and onto the main road. He spotted a lone figure walk towards him. The man was obese and well dressed. His short steps were hurried and his intent purposeful. He assessed the man to be a jeweller or a stock broker. There was every chance he would be carrying cash or something of value on him. Walsh approached his unfortunate victim and asked for directions to the railway station. The man appeared nervous and uncomfortable. He directed Walsh towards the station and continued on his way as fast as his adipose physique would permit. Walsh caught up, pressed his knife in the man's back and pushed him into a darkened doorway. The man begged and pleaded for mercy. Walsh patted the pleading man's pockets and relieved him of five hundred and fourteen rupees. He found two jewellery boxes, each containing a diamond ring. Walsh returned the boxes. This was not the time to be greedy. Jewellery was a traceable commodity. Walsh warned him with dire consequences if the man created a scene.

Thankful that he got away unharmed, the jeweller wasted no time in putting distance between him and the mugger. He waddled down the road without a glance over his shoulder. Walsh knew the man would file a complaint at the nearest police station. If the officer at the police station was a veteran he would receive assurances of a speedy recovery. But if the officer was a young enthusiastic rookie, he would start investigations immediately. That could prove to be a problem. The young enthusiast would commence his investigation from the scene of the crime and work his way to the station. Walsh chided himself for revealing his destination. Walsh headed for the station with his ill-gotten gains. He moved at a pace that would not draw attention. As he neared the end of the main road, the raucous sound of human revelry filled the air. The appetising aroma of street side cuisine urged him on. They stirred his gastric juices. A throng of youngsters jostled with one another next to the food stalls. He mingled with the unruly crowd and ate a little of everything on offer. Across the street were a row of shops selling lower quality ladies and gents garments. He bought a South African safari suit, a wide brimmed hat, boots and a cravat. He changed into the new clothes in a public toilet and discarded the old in a nearby rubbish dump. Well-fed and clad like a South African tourist, he felt confident to avoid the scrutiny of his fellow Englishmen. All he needed now were some cosmetic changes and he would be willing to look Holmes in the eye without a tremor.

Walsh surveyed the scene around the station before he entered to make enquiries. The absence of policemen indicated the hunt for him had not commenced. The activity in the reception area presented the normal hustle and bustle of stations everywhere.

He waited in the queue at the enquiry window, hoping to catch the first train heading for Bombay. He maintained a firm hold on the bag containing his precious statue. Highly skilful bag snatchers always hung around stations. In his khaki safari suit he looked like an amateur hunter at the end of an adventurous holiday. The man at the information window informed him that the earliest available train to Bombay would depart the following evening. It was a minor setback, but not one that could cause serious problems. He reserved a sleeping berth in the first class compartment. The fare to Bombay set him back quite a sum. Then he shopped for clothes more suitable for a first class passenger. His new jacket, shirt, necktie, trousers, shoes and a suitcase lent him the air of an upper middle class gentleman. He checked into a hotel across the road from the station. The balcony of his room offered a panoramic view of the station and its surroundings.

CHAPTER 17

The panel of enquiry comprised of a retired Supreme Court judge, the chief of police and Colonel Harvey. Their faces were grim and stern, their demeanour officious. Liam Crowe and Kamalbir Singh nervously waited for the interrogation to commence. The Supreme Court judge started the proceedings with a word of caution. He warned of severe penalties for half-truths and misleading statements. The judge chastised Crowe for his inexplicable absence during Travers's trip to the village and back. He ordered the detective to explain his absence. Crowe responded without hesitation. He knew that judges eyed dithering with suspicion. He described his absence as a tactical decision and assured the panel that they were within striking distance at all times. The judge found his explanation unacceptable. He reminded the inspector that he was nowhere to be seen when criminals attempted to kidnap Mister Travers or when he had a near fatal accident. Crowe explained that he and constable Singh left for the village a day earlier to make a preliminary survey of the area surrounding the temple. However he had arranged for a sizable police force to protect Mister Travers. Besides, they were confident that the colonel's considerable experience and ability would suffice. It had been a while since the colonel's achievements as a S.A.S. officer was acknowledged. However the compliment did nothing to assuage his dislike for the inspector. Crowe added that the governor had approved his plan. Harvey asked where they were at the time of the accident. Crowe explained that they were privy to information that underworld elements planned to kidnap Travers in the village. So they spent the night in a ruin in the woods scouring the area. The chief of police asked who supplied the information. Crowe declined to answer. He said it would jeopardise the safety of a reliable police informant and the credibility of the force. The panellists were slighted by Crowe's answer. The chief of police asked if Crowe suspected any of them to be informants of the underworld. The judge reminded him that they were members of her majesty's court of law. What is said here stays here.' Crowe succumbed to pressure and named the informant as Aslam.

Standing respectfully at the back of the room, Singh had tried his best to make sense of what each one said. The legal terms went way over his head. Having been warned not to speak unless he was directly questioned, he soon drifted into a world of his own. The mention of Aslam brought Singh back to the present with a jolt. The mention of any of the don's men to the upholders of law spelt trouble. The man was ruthless and merciless when dealing with his enemies. The defenders of the law were top of his list of enemies. The man had informants in every government office. If he learned of this, he would move heaven and earth to learn the source. If he learnt that Kamalbir Singh was present, it could be the end of him and his family. Crowe had nothing to fear. He had never even seen Aslam. Crowe had only learnt of the name from him.

Harvey was bent on trapping Crowe. He raised the question of Crowe's stolen car. Crowe admitted that he had parked the car away from the hospital as he feared any of the don's gangsters being aware of his presence. Harvey asked if the don's men frequented the missionary hospital. Crowe did not reply.

Getting nowhere with Crowe, the panel decided to question Singh. The head constable stood sweating, squirming, fidgeting and constantly shifting his weight from one leg to the other. He remained preoccupied with the consequences of the don's vengeance. The panel watched him for a while mildly amused.

'Are you alright constable Singh?' The chief of police asked. The mention of his name caught Singh off guard. Crowe heaved a sigh of relief. For the first time the spotlight had shifted away from him. He had a pretty good idea of how the interrogation with Singh would end.

'Huh' Singh uttered and then quickly corrected himself. 'I am sorry sir. I mean I beg your pardon sir. I mean----.' His usual confusion of the English language twisted his brain in knots. He stood gaping at the panel, silent and attentive.

The chief of police repeated his question. 'Are you well constable?'

'Yes sir, I am very well sir, thank you sir.'

'Then why are you behaving like a bally Egyptian dancer with an epileptic fit?'

'I don't know any Egyptians or belly dancers, sir. But I am very fit sir, thank you sir.'

Even the humourless judge could not supress a smile.

'Where were you at the time of the temple celebrations?'

'I was firmly on chief inspector Crowe's back sir.'

The chief of police sensed a chance to trap Crowe by questioning this half-witted constable.

'Why did you park the car in the field?'

'I did not park the car in the field sir, Inspector Crowe did.'

'Did you go into the temple?'

'No sir, I am a Sikh by birth. I only go to a Gurdwara every week.'

The panel of judges sighed in unison. 'It's no use. Reverend Beech warned me about this man's limited understanding of the English language' Harvey whispered so as not to offend Singh.

The retired judge put an end to the comedy talk show. 'That'll be all' he said. 'This is not going to lead us anywhere.' The three men panel huddled together to discuss the outcome of the trial. Harvey wished to continue in the hope of trapping the constable on some minor detail about Crowe's recent failure. The chief of police too insisted they continue the interrogation. The judge confirmed that they had no evidence of criminal involvement or deliberate neglect on the part of Crowe or Singh. He pronounced his judgement. 'We find you guilty of gross mismanagement of duties and negligence. The matter will be put on hold for now. If any fresh evidence comes to light, you will be called up for further questioning.'

The chief of police found himself in a bind. Pressure from the top to arrest the perpetrator was mounting with every passing day. A freshly appointed officer would need time to get fully acquainted with the case. The replacement would need to start from scratch. Crowe was the only one familiar with every aspect of the case. For want of a better alternative, he decided to permit Crowe to continue pursuing the case. He hoped Crowe would deliver a positive outcome.

CHAPTER 18

Walsh paced the floor of his hotel room like a caged animal. He worried about the possibility of the stolen car being found. It would not take long to trace the owner. Once the owner revealed the place of the theft, the police would know the perpetrator was in Calcutta. Then there was the matter of the mugged jeweller or moneylender. The hippo would reveal that the mugger had asked for directions to the station. The station would turn into a well-guarded fortress. A massive manhunt would commence. Trains could be indefinitely delayed. He took solace in the fact that his mugged victim could not provide an accurate description. As he paced the floor he nervously fidgeted with many large and small items. Without consciously wanting to, he moved pieces of furniture around. He kicked aside a small three legged table for continuously getting in his way. He opened the cupboard door and gaped stupidly at the empty shelves. The tension left him mentally exhausted. He lay on the bed and almost immediately drifted into a deep slumber.

Walsh dreamt he was standing on a raised bank of a river. Everything around him was seeped in an eerie red glow. The statue was firmly clasped against his chest. The deafening sound of rushing water far below filled the air. Leafless stumps of dead rotting trees lined the river on both sides. They seemed to watch his every move like sentinels from hell. The suffocating stench of blood permeated the air. Suddenly, the earth below him gave way. He tumbled into a dark and seemingly bottomless abyss and plunged noiselessly into the flowing river. The statue remained firmly in his grasp. The gushing torrent threatened to drown him. It sloshed and swirled around him, carrying him forward with demonic force. He could taste the revolting blood, yet he felt the desire to wallow in it. The tree stumps swayed like in some bizarre ritual dance. He felt their cold clammy touch as they nudged him onward. Their shrill eerie laughter sounded like the death cries of a thousand tortured souls. In the distance a glowing crimson ball manifested out of nowhere. He stared at it, transfixed by its evil power. He watched it transform into something much more sinister. It seemed to possess hypnotic powers. He could not get himself to look away. The river of blood roared its way towards the apparition. A beam shot out of two dark discs aimed directly at him. It compelled him to let the bloody river carry him towards the sinister apparition. He lacked the strength to fight against its influence. He found himself racing towards the fearsome creature. Suddenly a blissful calm descended on the hell surrounding him. A brilliant beam of light pierced through the depressing veil of darkness. Soft angelic voices rose above the deafening roar of the river and the shrill eerie cries of the trees. Angels appeared in the beam of heavenly light. The angels hovered directly over his head, singing soul soothing hymns. The angels gently urged him to relinquish his treasure. The heavenly light and the soothing hymns filled him with blissful joy. He stretched out his arms to hand over the statue. A thunderous below drowned the angelic hymns. A battle waged between the hymns and the roar. He covered his ears to shut out the cacophonic confusion. The fiery apparition appeared all the more hideous. A feeling of dread washed over him. His will to relinquish the statue died. A gigantic shimmering sword whirled through the air towards him. It had the face of Lucifer on the hilt. A shrill voice ordered him to cut the heavenly beam. His mind was a maelstrom of confusion. Bewildered and petrified, he grabbed the sword and slashed the air. The blade severed the beam. The vision of the angels vanished. The crimson ball of fire roared with laughter. The cavernous abyss opened wider. He was swallowed by the hideous beast.

Walsh awoke with a start, drenched in sweat. He peered wide eyed into the darkness of the unfamiliar room. The devilish apparition stood in one corner with its hideous cavernous mouth wide open. He stared helplessly at it. Mustering courage, he jumped out of bed and mindlessly kicked out at the hideous creature. His foot struck its tentacles. They collapsed inwards with a loud bang and struck back with equal force, throwing him on the bed. The blow brought sense and reason to his partially deranged mind. With trembling hands he managed to light the bedside candle. The glow brought the unfamiliar room into focus. The cupboard gaped back at him with its doors wide open. Sleep had deserted him. He resumed his pacing.

Walsh splashed his face with icy cold water. Sleep was impossible after the nightmare. He looked at his watch. It read, five thirty in the morning. He dressed, packed, paid his dues and stepped out of the hotel in the wee hours of the morning. A cheap all-night café offered an unrestricted view of the activity around the station. Walsh closely studied the scene in and around the entrance of the station. The unruly throng of humanity indicated that no restrictions were in place yet.

CHAPTER 19

Crowe sat at his office desk looking miserable. His job and his reputation were on the line. The panel of vultures had granted him a reprieve. But he knew that Harvey and the chief were circling above like vultures, waiting for him to fall by the wayside. Had he the means, he would have gladly packed up and quit his job. But he hadn't saved a penny. Above all, he grieved for the loss of his precious car.

Crowe found it hard to concentrate. He read and reread the synopsis he had made of the village crime, hoping for an overlooked clue. His efforts yielded nothing. He turned his attention to reports of crimes in the city. A mugging in the industrial section of Calcutta bothered him. It wasn't headline news. Muggings in that part of the city were a common occurrence. A junior policeman entered his cabin and revealed that his car had been found in the industrial part of town. The key was still in it. For a while his elation hampered his ability to think logically. Something about where the car was found started to niggle at his brain. Finally he made the connection. The car was found in the vicinity of the mugging. He conclude that the perpetrator of all three crimes were one and the same person. He needed more proof. He reread the complaint of the mugged victim for the third time. Crowe used the mugging as the hypothesis to start his investigation. He was aware he was taking a shot in the dark. But then, desperate situations called for desperate measures.

On the strength of the mugged victim's report, Crowe concentrated his attention on the railway station. He studied the schedule of arrivals and departures. The Calcutta Jhansi express was due to leave at five thirty that evening. It would end its journey in Central India. The Delhi bound train was due to leave at six. A number of trains for closer destinations departed every morning and evening. He decided to place his best detectives on platforms of trains leaving for Delhi and Jhansi.

Commuters along with their friends and family arrived in droves. The scene resembled a pilgrimage to the Kumbh Mela. Checking every commuter would be a Herculean task. He separated the commuters of each train and divided them by the class they were travelling. Those travelling by third class comprised almost entirely of poor native Indians. They were capable of turning violent. He decided to let them enter the station first. Crowe ordered his men to concentrate on male passengers travelling by first and second class. Anyone raising the slightest suspicion was to be questioned. He knew the upper crust would create a fuss. But this was not a run of the mill luggage check. Considering who and what was involved, even the viceroy would be willing to permit his luggage to be inspected.

****

Walsh returned from his shopping spree an hour before departure time. He settled down at the café. The detectives stood out like sore thumbs. They stood motionless like trees, closely watching people pass by. Their stance stank of police academy. There was no attempt to try and blend in with the crowd. They all seemed to focus their attentions on passing white males. He would need to keep a close watch on all of them at the same time. Walsh turned his attention to the activities around the entrance. The ticket inspector appeared far too alert for a railway employee. He was the only one of his species, more interested in the passengers than the tickets. The man was beyond doubt a policeman in ticket inspector's clothing. A Sikh giant stood by ticket inspector, erect and attentive. A flicker of recognition sparked his memory cells into action. He had definitely seen the man before now. He relived the days since Christopher's holy ritual in the village. He recalled the turbaned officer's presence at the temple. He remembered seeing the giant Sikh follow an Irish inspector like the tail of a dog. He wondered if the Irish inspector was also present at the station. His eyes fell on a short chubby man next to the Sikh. The overweight pigmy was easy to recognise. They had met on a lonely stretch of road not too long ago. The man's presence turned his blood cold. Would the pigmy recognise him? He doubted it. He had taken care not to expose his full face to the victim. It was a gamble he would have to take. Preoccupied with identifying probable difficulties, he had failed to notice that the disorderly rush of passengers had morphed into disciplined lines of commuters. Each line was supervised by a group of policemen. He decided to take his chances and approach the station.

****

The upper class were offended by the preference given to the third class passengers. The blistering sun only made matters worse. Tempers flared, objections were barked out in harsh tones and insults were directed at the authorities. Crowe sensed the mood and ordered the process be speeded up. A distinguished looking man pushed past his fellow passengers and confronted the ticket inspector. The irate man was tall, well-built and in no mood to be dictated to by a government employee. He was prepared to take on any and everybody who dared to defy him.

He produced his ticket from his jacket pocket and thrust it under the ticket inspector's nose. He entered the main hall without permission. A short overweight man standing close by threw a tizzy fit. He pointed to the aristocratic Englishman and emitted a shrill cry to stop the man. His cry carried over the din of the crowd. The irate aristocrat glared at the human ball of lard. Singh grabbed on to the arm of the irate Englishman. The Englishman punched Singh in the chest and shouted 'Get your filthy paws off me you bloody gorilla.' Singh was unsure of how to handle the situation. He was trained not to man handled an Englishman. This was uncharted territory for him. The incensed man's fuss attracted everyone's attention. Torn between duty and etiquette, Singh tightened his grip on to the man's arm. Much to his relief Crowe appeared on the scene and profusely apologised. His manner was polite yet firm.

The exchange of words between the aristocrat and the Crowe threatened to turn ugly. They were in the midst of a heated argument when Harvey arrived on the scene. He pushed past Crowe and addressed the man with courtesy that chilled Crowe to the bone. Harvey introduced himself and shook the man's hand. Noticing the perplexed look on the man's face, Harvey reminded the man that they had met at the governor's home recently. He turned and introduced the man to Crowe. 'This is Sir Mortimer Davis, a guest and close friend of His Excellency the governor.' Crowe turned as white as a sheet.

All through the fracas, the remaining first and second class passengers were left to roast in the blistering heat. They took matters into their own hands. En mass, they stormed the entrance like a marauding army of Huns. The sheer force of the crowd overwhelmed the police guarding the gate. Chaos ruled supreme in the entrance hall. The pandemonium made it impossible to mind the entrance. Crowe decided to let everyone through and shift the inspection to the platform entrance.

****

Walsh silently thanked the incensed Englishman for the ruckus. He joined the marauding horde and entered the station. Walsh headed straight for the platform entrance. An elderly gentleman reprimanded him for not letting a coolie carry his luggage. He said it under minded the image of the English rulers. Walsh recalled the unwritten rule of English passengers. He reluctantly handed his bag to a passing coolie. For the first time since he left the temple, he and the Goddess had been apart. It felt like he had lost a limb. Walsh was relieved to note that he was no longer the focus of attention. He bought sandwiches, samosas and a flask full of tea. He would need it if he was forced to travel in the luggage compartment. The hamper would sustain him at least till they reached Jhansi. He even bought a cup of tea for the coolie to ensure that the man did not disappear into the crowd with his precious statue. He wondered what the coolie's reaction would be, if he knew what he was carrying on his head. The thought amused him.

The platform entrance was barricaded by policemen and ticket inspectors. Walsh noticed that the giant Sikh and the Irish inspector were missing. He could not risk either one of them recognising him. The scene at the platform entrance was far more orderly than at the main gate. Walsh waited patiently, studying the modus operandi of the minders of the platform entrance. Passengers were being permitted through the gate only after being bombarded by a series of questions. At first the authorities demanded proof of the passenger's identity. Once again, those minding the gate became the target of temper tantrums of the upper crust. Many regarded the demand of identity proof as an insult. Some asked if the ticket inspectors suspected them of being criminals. Others took umbrage and asked if India had turned into a police state. They vociferously complained that they were being treated as common criminals. An elderly gentleman blocked the platform entrance by sitting on his suitcase and defying them to try and move him. He refused to budge no matter how much they pleaded and apologised. Passengers waiting behind the defiant gentleman backed him up. The authorities were forced to change their approach. The outraged elderly gentleman was permitted through without question or inspection. The other passengers were merely asked their names, destinations and reason for travel. The detectives stood by, searching for any signs of suspicious behaviour.

Walsh observed that true to form, the railway staff and junior police were getting bored, careless and lax. They only checked the tickets as they were accustomed to doing. Walsh permitted a few more of his fellow passengers to go ahead before he stepped into the queue. The unexpected arrival of the Irish inspector made him edgy. He had no option but to chance it. An overzealous young detective stopped him with a gesture of the hand. He gave the tall gaunt passenger a once over. Walsh glared back, making the detective more than a little anxious. The rookie asked his name, his occupation and his destination. Then, unsure of what to do with the information, he merely waved him through. 'Good work, keep it up' Walsh said, patting the rookie's arm.

The platform lacked the usual frantic activity. The passengers were ordered to go directly to their allotted berths and remain inside the carriage at all times. Constables maintained a constant vigil. Walsh sat by the window, observing the platform. He spotted a khaki turban floating in the air. Under it was the monolithic Sikh. The turban was in the company of two men. One of them was the enigmatic Irishman. They walked at a pace that would have exasperated a tortoise on a lazy afternoon stroll. He tensed as they passed by his carriage. All three men glanced in his direction but appeared disinterested. Only the monolithic Sikh kept his eyes fixed on him. Alarm bells rang out loud in Walsh's head. The trio moved on. He watched them walk to the final second class carriage and turn. Fear gripped Walsh. He kept his eyes peeled on them. They were inching closer to his carriage. An announcement, ordering all senior policemen to be present at the station entrance saved the day. He watched them hurry towards the main gate.

****

Duty compelled Singh to accompany Crowe and Harvey to the main gate of the station. His seniors fell into conversation with other senior officers. Singh felt ignored. He hung around for a while. The face he had noticed in one of the carriages continued to niggle. He was sure he had seen the face somewhere. He wanted to take a second look. Singh returned to the platform in search of the mystery man. He headed for the carriage where he had noticed the familiar face. The mystery man was not in the carriage. He stood by the carriage and scanned the platform. Halfway down the platform he spotted a tall Englishman carrying a small suitcase and a satchel. The man's behaviour was suspicious. He continuously looked over his shoulder. He seemed to be in a desperate hurry. Singh followed the suspicious character. A group of children decided to play some absurd game around him. Their tomfoolery caused him to lose sight of his quarry. Singh hurried in the direction of the engine. His height helped him to see over the heads of the crowd. It dawned on him that his quarry was an Englishman. He had never questioned let alone arrested a sahib. He decided to request the assistance of one of the detectives stationed on the platform.

Every so often, Singh was forced to step aside to avoid colliding with other passengers. Try as he might, he could not locate his quarry. Undeterred, Singh continued his search. A group of middle-aged ladies, delighted to bump into one another blocked his path. The constant impediment was starting to irritate him. Frustrated, Singh stopped at a tea stall for a cup of masala chai. The steaming sweet brew aided his memory cells. He recalled the man was present at the temple during Travers's visit. Now Singh needed the assistance of a senior more than ever. He had identified the criminal. Unable to spot the suspect on the platform, he decided to search the compartments. He entered each carriage at one end and exited at the other. His efforts were in vain. In the three carriages he had inspected, he saw no one even vaguely resembling his quarry. But Singh was convinced he was not chasing a figment of his imagination.

Detective Mather stood on the platform, annoyed by the futility of Crowe's plan. Bored to tears, he idly stood around watching the public go by. His attention was drawn to a sight that offered a bit of amusement. He noticed constable Singh jump in and out of three carriages. The detective knew the constable well. He was sure that Singh had a perfectly good reason for his absurd behaviour. Mather's curiosity got the better of him. He approached Singh and questioned him. Singh related the events that led him to identify the criminal. It piqued the detective's interest. Mather was prepared to investigate the vaguest lead. The detective offered to join Singh in quest.

****

The length of the platform seemed to be unending. After what felt like a marathon walk Walsh arrived within proximity of the goods carriage. He was mentally physically exhausted. Walsh did not enter the parcel carriage immediately. He noticed a detective watching the activity with undistracted attention. Walsh deftly kept a group of passengers between him and the hawk. He noticed the hawk fixedly watching something behind him. He turned his head and followed the detective's stare. Walsh's heart skipped a beat. The Sikh was just two carriages behind him. Walsh had no option but to stand where he was and hope for the best. The hawk approached the Sikh and fell into a conversation. Walsh took advantage of the distraction. He peered into the goods carriage and quickly pulled back. A gang of labourers were busy arranging crates and boxes. He entered the passenger carriage next to the goods carriage, keeping an eye on the hawk and the Sikh.

A stream of commuters barged into the carriage. He was forced to press himself against the bulkhead and let them enter. His eyes fell on the Sikh entering the other end of his carriage. The turban very nearly touched the roof of the car. Walsh felt trapped. The giant was weaving his way past the other passengers. There was no telling where the hawk might be. His brain seemed to have gone dead. Ideas and stratagems that had helped him in the past now abandoned him. He desperately looked for an escape route. Walsh noticed the Delhi bound train waiting on the neighbouring platform. The doors of the carriages were open. Walsh jumped onto the tracks and scrambled into the Delhi bound train. He hoped he had given the two hounds the slip. But he was not prepared to be complacent. The most dangerous element of the escapade lay ahead. He would need to reach the parcel car of his train before its departure. If the two hounds were anywhere around the game was up. The statue was proving to be cumbersome. He toyed with the idea of abandoning the statue in the event the chase got too hot. The thought was too upsetting to contemplate. He was prepared to fight to the bitter end. Worse come to worse, he was prepared to leap under the Jhansi express and end it all. Life without any money was worse than purgatory.

Singh and Mather were perplexed. The detective refused to accept defeat. He looked around him and noticed the Delhi train. It aroused the detective's suspicions. Mather told Singh to leap across the tracks and board the Delhi bound train. Singh did exactly as he was told. Mather decided to go around the Jhansi train's engine and reach the Delhi train's platform. Singh jumped into the Delhi with ease. Mather was confident he had the criminal in his grasp. Mather and Singh approached the carriage from either end. Once again the criminal seemed to have vanished into thin air.

****

Walsh saw the turban jump onto the tracks and board the neighbouring carriage. As long as he knew the Sikh's whereabouts he knew he was ahead of the game. Walsh eased himself onto the tracks and cautiously made his way towards the engine of the Jhansi train. He heard someone jump onto the tracks behind him. Walsh peered from behind the engine. The Sikh too had descended onto the tracks. But the Sikh climbed into the Jhansi train. He feared the detective could be waiting on platform one. Walsh peeped from behind the engine and scanned the platform. He saw no sign of the hawk. He scrambled up the luggage ramp and hurried to the goods carriage. The carriage was empty. He entered and crouched between two large crates. Moments later someone closed the doors.

****

Singh saw Walsh climb down onto the tracks. He decided to give chase. He leapt onto the tracks with creditable agility and stopped. He faced a dilemma. He could either follow the criminal round the engine or use the Jhansi train to cut him off. He decided on the second option. He scrambled into the Jhansi carriage. His hurried footsteps sounded like thunder. Singh was confident he had the criminal in his clutches. Images of him being showered with awards, accolades and a promotion raced through his mind. He could picture Crowe squirming with envy. He was almost out of the carriage when he heard a firm authoritative voice order him to stop. Singh froze like Lot's wife. This was not just a voice of your everyday sahib. This was the voice of sophistication and authority. He turned to face a dapper gentleman of less than average height. The top of the dapper gentleman's head just about reached his chest. Singh fixed his gaze on a spot above and beyond the gentleman's head.

'Do you have no concern for others? Your footsteps resemble a herd of stampeding cattle. Can you read English?'

'Yes sir'

'Then you must be aware that this is a reserved carriage. It is clearly written on the door.'

'I am looking for a man sir.'

'And you find that a rare commodity in a crowded station?'

'Yes sir, no sir.' Singh found the question confusing.

'Look at me when you speak.' The voice was soft, but the order was firm.

Singh bent his neck to see the face of his interrogator. He found himself looking into the face of the chief justice of the Calcutta high court. The man was notorious for meeting out harsh punishments for the most trivial offences. Trepidation gripped Singh. He was not a man of tears, but he felt he might weep at any moment. He started to stammer out an explanation but the public announcement system burst into life. It informed all who could follow the garbled sound of the imminent departure of the Jhansi express. 'You are dismissed' the judge barked and returned to his compartment. Singh's dream of medals and accolades came crashing down all around him. He feared that the criminal might have slipped out of his grasp. Mather joined Singh on the Jhansi platform. The detective and Singh stood and watched as the Jhansi express disappeared into the distance. 'I am convinced that somewhere on that train is a priceless statue and the murderer of two innocent people' the detective said. They walked in silence towards the station's main gate to join Crowe.

CHAPTER 20

Crowe contemplated the consequences of his failure. Termination of his job was inevitable. It depressed him. He possessed no other skills. He wondered if they would give him a pension. The appearance of Singh did nothing to boost his sprits. He eyed his chief constable with concern. The man looked just as sullen and depressed. He too appeared to be lost in some private melancholia of his own.

'What's eating you? Your job is not on the line.'

Singh looked sullenly at his boss like a child who has lost his puppy. He moaned and groaned about letting the criminal slip out of his grasp.

Crowe willed himself to remain calm. He reminded himself that Singh was endowed with the brain of a honeybadger. Once an idea entered his dense head, it stayed there. Singh went on to explain how detective Mather and he had the criminal trapped. Had the chief justice not interfered, the criminal and the statue would have been in the palm of his hands. The inclusion of the chief justice and Mather made Crowe pause and think. Mather was a first class detective.

Crowe recognised that Singh had inadvertently thrown him a lifeline. This was his final chance to redeem himself. He recalled that Jhansi was a military stronghold. Therefore any request or order from him or the chief of police would go unheeded. Crowe used persuasion and manipulation to convince the governor to issue an order for an intensive inspection of the passengers at Jhansi. Considering that the viceroy was personally involved in the case, the governor had no option but to comply. Crowe endured forty eight tense hours waiting for word from Jhansi.

CHAPTER 21

Walsh waited till the doors of the parcel carriage slammed shut. Alone in an enclosed, dark, hot and humid place, he felt claustrophobic and uneasy. He experienced first-hand what criminals of medieval times felt when incarcerated in dark and dingy dungeons. Irrational thoughts filled him with dread. Fearful images of the priest's ghost plagued his thoughts. However, he had no choice but to endure. He had taken the plunge. The choice was to cross the river or drown. He forced his mind to dwell on positive thoughts.

The train jerked, heaved and crawled out of the station. The iron horse strained to gather momentum. Sunbeams penetrated the narrow slits in the bulkhead, creating a mosaic of weird patterns. The wind whistled through the cracks, sounding like the howls of demons and wolves. He wolfed down two samosas and as many sandwiches and washed it down with a cup of tea. He stretched out and drifted into the world of reminiscence. Strange scrapping sounds invaded his thoughts. They seemed out of place. He struck a match and looked about him. Everything was as it should be. The flame went out, leaving him cloaked in semi-darkness. The mysterious scrapping sound returned. This time it was accompanied by high pitched squeaks. They seemed to emanate from somewhere beyond the realm of the living. He forced himself to ignore the sound and concentrate on his immediate problems. He would face a lot of problems in Bombay. Everyone from railway officials to vendors and urchins knew him. If just one of them recognised him, all his troubles would be in vain. Something small fell into his lap. He started and brushed it away. Moments later the parcel returned. He grabbed it and angrily threw it across the carriage. A high pitched squeak followed a thud as the parcel struck a crate. The scraping sound resumed. It convinced him that it was an out of the world creature. His imagination went into overdrive. Was the village priest seeking revenge? Was the Goddess making him pay for his sins? Walsh sat huddled in a corner, waiting for an opportunity escape from the hellhole.

The wheels screeched and the train jolted to a halt. He peeped through a crack in the bulkhead. The outside was too dark to tell where he was. The carriage doors opened with an ear-splitting screech. A gang of cargo handler's entered, holding a lantern before them. The labourers proceeded to unload boxes. Walsh stood to flee from the hellhole. The cargo handlers stood frozen, gaping at the apparition. They abandoned their chores and fled with their tails in the grooves. A rat scampered away into the shadows, squeaking his approval of the stranger's departure. Walsh eyed the ill lit platform. He seemed to be the only one up and about. He started to walk towards his allotted carriage. A station master approached from his left and questioned him. Walsh gave him a cock and bull explanation. The station master looked at him, poker faced. He was clearly not buying Walsh's story. He asked to see Walsh's ticket. It was more an order than a request. Walsh produced the ticket and handed it over. The sight of a first class ticket altered the man's attitude. He ushered the passenger to his carriage.

Walsh heaved a sigh of relief as he lowered his overtaxed body into the comfortable well-padded seat. He was glad to be out of the hellhole. He could now relax. The passengers were fast asleep. Some lifted their heads and looked sleepily at the newcomer. He was spared the vexation of quizzical stares and inquisitive questions. But he knew it would not last long. Come morning the gapers and interrogators would be up and about. The stares and questions would commence. Experience had taught him the best way to deal with the inquisitive would be to return their stares with stern glares. He would answer questions with curt responses. It never failed to quell their curiosity.

The unnerving experience in the cargo carriage had robbed him of sleep. A succession of thoughts and memories raced through his mind. He relived the incident in the temple. The thought of surrendering to the authorities crossed his mind. Of course, he would need to convince one and all that the priest was already dead when he entered the temple. That would be difficult but not impossible. Magistrates were a wily and shrewd breed. One slip and he could head straight for the gallows. The very thought of courts and judges induced a change of heart. A lot has been said about God's infinite capacity to forgive. But that was not true about judges. They were a notoriously cold and unforgiving lot.

His thoughts wandered off into the future. Bombay was less than two days away. It was a city he knew like the back of his hand. He decided to head straight for Chin Min's opium den. The dealer of stolen artefacts never failed to visit the place. Dealers always commenced the bargaining at half the true price. That would give him a fair idea of its value. After much haggling, they would seal the deal with a handshake. Walsh imagined himself walking away a rich man. He would acquire a new identity. He decided on settling down in far off Australia. An employee of the dining car disturbed his reverie. His fellow passengers stretched, yawned and hurried off to relieve and refresh themselves. In another few hours they would reach Jhansi. Walsh prepared to disembark on a station that he hoped would be free of problems and policemen.

Walsh was relieved to see the absence of policemen on Jhansi station. However, armed military personnel marched purposefully up and down the platform. The passengers who alighted from the Calcutta train were being told to proceed to the B.B. & C.I platform on the other side of a barren tract of land. A flat featureless walkway ran through its centre. The military personnel watched the passengers like hawks. The Bombay bound train waited on the other side of it. Walsh waited by his carriage door studying the scene. A military officer ordered Walsh to move on. Walsh pretended to suffer from breathing difficulty. The officer moved away, leaving Walsh to solve the problem on his own.

Walsh studied the modus operandi of the military. The third class passengers were made to board the train first. They were being herded in like cattle. Men with families and the old and infirm were the next to board the connecting train. Caucasian males travelling alone had their luggage meticulously searched. They also suffered the indignity of being intensely interrogated. The military personnel in Jhansi were doing a far better job than the Calcutta police. He had to find a way to get into the connecting train without being searched. He did not so much mind being questioned, but a search was unthinkable. Walsh shuffled along the walkway and sat down smack dab in the middle of the walkway. He complained of giddiness and laboured breathing. Fellow commuters gathered round. Some knelt to offer him water, others called out for help. The smooth flow of passengers was disrupted. A military man rudely ordered the crowd around Walsh to move on. His attitude upset the ladies. They flew at the officer in unison. The officer had been trained to deal with people from behind a gun. He was nonplussed. He was too young and too naïve to deal with infuriated women. The soldier said he was merely acting on orders of the commanding officer. The passengers dismissed his explanation. One woman threatened to take him and the entire British military to court for inhuman behaviour, if the ailing man died. The soldier's superior officer arrived on the scene sporting a thick handlebar moustache. He spoke politely but with authority. The horde of ladies gave him an earful for the young soldier's callous attitude. Much to his amusement, Walsh was carried like a maharaja across the walkway by two railway employees. He was deposited in his allotted seat, no questions asked. He even found the courage to demand they bring him some tea. The train's booming whistle was followed by that of the guard. The train jerked to a start. Walsh was on the final leg of his eventful journey to Bombay. More importantly, he was on his way to realising his dream.

CHAPTER 22

Walsh sat in the first class compartment, enjoying the comforts that came with it. The mildly cool pre-monsoon air was a bonus. He had not felt so relaxed since he stepped out of the temple. It all seemed such a very long time ago. He sank into a dreamless sleep after a heavy lunch. The ear splitting cry of a vendor, standing just outside his window shook him out of his slumber. Given the opportunity, Walsh would have gladly decapitated the vendor and buried him with his wares. A group of teenage girls burst into laughter. 'Aren't you Sylvia Walsh's son?' a middle aged lady asked. The question hit him like a speeding train. He was so taken aback that he found his brain fumbling to answer the simple question. 'No madam' he said at last. My name is James Cobb.' That was the only uncomfortable moment he experienced during the entire journey.

The train crawled into Victoria terminus station in the wee hours of the morning. It kissed the buffers and loudly sighed to a halt. The familiar smells and sounds of the city rushed to greet him. He felt apprehensive. He kept a keen lookout for familiar faces. People are known to have the bad habit of turning up wherever and whenever they are least wanted. The absence of police was a relief. The station clock read twelve minutes past three in the morning. He calculated that Chin Min's opium den was an hour's walk from the station. Chin Min would make an entrance around nine in the morning. But that did not pose a problem. The staff knew him well. He was confident of a warm welcome.

A bottleneck of passengers crowded the exit. The ticket inspectors did not perform their duties in their usual lackadaisical manner. He was not willing to chance the canny efficiency of the Bombay police. Walsh recalled a side entrance that facilitated the entry and exit of railway staff. He looked around to ensure that no one was watching him. He slipped out of the entrance unnoticed.

Walsh left the station area and made his way to Frayre road. At the far end of Frayre road, past Alexandra docks and prince's docks was an area known as Carnac Bunder. It was the melting pot of crime. Chin Min's infamous opium den lay on its outskirts. Due to the day and night activities of the docks, Frayre road remained perpetually crowded. He would be just another man among hundreds with a bag. Once past the two docks, it would take roughly twenty to twenty five minutes to reach the den. A light drizzle added to his woes. He knew of a narrow by lane that would considerably reduce walking time. The lane was a night time refuge for beggars and street urchins. No gaslights illuminated the entire length of the lane. It was free of muggers and other criminals. Walsh turned into the by lane warily. A nauseating stench greeted him the moment he entered. His eyes constantly darted from side to side. Pigs, stray dogs, drunks, dope addicts and beggars eyed him suspiciously as he walked past. Rats the size of rabbits scampered about, foraging for scraps. They hissed angrily to keep the suspicious intruder at bay. They were not eager to share the refuse with anyone. The gentle drizzle morphed into a heavy downpour. It reduced visibility. The darkness started to play tricks with his mind. He was halfway into the lane when he noticed movement in the shadows. Walsh stopped in his strides and drew his knife from his boot. His heart beat like a jungle drum. Mustering all his courage, he resumed his walk to the end of the lane. Frayre road was roughly fifty yards ahead of him.

The glow of a streetlamp on the main road dimly illuminated the end of the lane. All else was shrouded in darkness. Piles of garbage lay on either side of the lane. They seemed to tower ten feet in the air. An eerie apparition manifested itself out of the garbage pile and spoke in a rasping voice. The hair on the nape of Walsh's neck stood on end. His limbs shook like tuning forks and his brain was a muddled mess of fear and confusion. As he stared at the fiendish creature it assumed human form. It attempted to block his path with an outstretched arm. Walsh avoided any eye contact. He broke into a run. He repeatedly glanced over his shoulder. The spectre from hell was following him. Mind numbing fear took hold of him. The murdered priest crossed his mind. He was damned if he would let the pesky phantom have its way. He was even prepared to fight the priest's spirit. The terrifying creature was gaining on him with its tentacle like arm held in front of him. It was trying to snatch the bag from him? It seemed to have magically shrunk in size. It continued to dog him, emitting an eerie rasping sound. He held on to his bag as tightly as possible. Mindlessly he sprinted onto the main road throwing glances over his shoulder. A hideous sound, like that of a braying mule cut through the night air. He turned to see a four legged monster with enormous shining eyes charge at him. Its grin displayed hideously long silvery teeth. In his state of panic he stepped right into its path. The fiendish beast rammed into him with the force of a charging rogue elephant. Its heavy body rolled over him. A trickle of blood oozed out of the side of his mouth. And then there was nothing.

****

The beggar stood at the end of the lane baffled by the sequence of events. He did not mean to scare the dead man. All he wanted were a few petty coins to buy him tea and chapatti. All day his brain and body was crying out for sustenance. When he heard approaching footsteps, he rose from his bed of garbage in the hope of receiving a little something. Never had he known of one who was prepared to kill himself, rather than part with a few coins. The beggar gaped at the dead Englishman, stupefied. The headlights of a passing car drew his attention to the suitcase. It was heavy. He returned to the sanctuary of the lane, clinging to his latest acquisition. He hoped there would be something in the bag to see him through another day. He knew he had to vacate the area immediately. If he was caught with the bag of a dead Englishman, a long sentence or the gallows awaited him.

The first thing the beggar noticed was an oilcloth bundle. It roused his curiosity. He starred at the shimmering statue in awe and wonder. He wondered if the gold and jewels were real. He erased the thought from his mind. The Goddess had chosen to come to him. He would worship and serve her loyally for the rest of his life.

The beggar's native village of Vajeshwari lay some forty miles from the city. It was named after a saintly soul who resided there with her two sisters, eons ago. After they abandoned their earthly bodies, a temple was erected there in their memory. The village also boasted of a spa. The villagers believed that the deity had created the springs to take a hot bath. True or not, the water was surely blessed. It cured the ailing and infirm. In time it attracted a large number of folks from Bombay and as far afield as Surat. Now the village would also be blessed with a temple of Goddess Laxmi. His parents died when he was just seven years old. His paternal uncle's widow sold him to a couple from Bombay, visiting the spa. They promised to pay him well if he worked well. For six years he slogged for no pay and little food. One night, he managed to escape with five rupees he stole from the heartless couple's cupboard. On the strength of what he considered a king's ransom he scoured the city for employment. Either he was too young, too frail or simply unsuitable for any of the jobs. In the course of a month the five rupees dwindled to a few petty coins. Begging was his only remaining option. He suffered verbal and physical abuse. Once, a fellow beggar attacked him with a knife for a loaf of stale bread. He had to flee from that area. After ten long years of abject misery, the Goddess Laxmi decided to take pity on him.

The beggar sold the bag and the clothes in Bombay's infamous Chor Bazaar. A beggar carrying an expensive suitcase would attract undue attention. He replaced the oilcloth wrapping with an old dhoti. No one paid him the slightest heed as he boarded the train. The beggar alighted at Bassien station. A lot had changed since he first travelled to Bombay. From Bassien there were several modes of transport to reach his village. The bullock cart was the slowest but the cheapest. The cart was crammed to bursting point with the poorest commuters. After several hours of bouncing and churning they arrived at his native village. He failed to spot a single familiar face. Strangers occupied what was once his uncle's home. No one recognised him. No one cared to enquire or hear the tale of his troubled past. The only good news he received was that his uncle's wife had suffered a painful death. By sheer chance he happened to run into his old schoolmaster in the market. He was the only one who recognised him as his ex-student Ramoo. The evening shadows spread across the village. The schoolmaster permitted him to spend the night in the school shed. Over dinner he revealed all.

The teacher had a shed erected next to the school. It served as a temple and the beggar's residence. Ramoo was employed as a sweeper in the school. Time trudged by at a painfully slow pace. Every weekend a handful of worshipers would visit the shed. The statue was placed behind a fishnet curtain. The visitors only got a sense of the Goddess's presence. They left behind a bit of small change. He managed to get by on his salary. The meagre earnings from the temple remained untouched. Diwali season was upon them. The village was invaded by visitors from nearby towns and cities. It was the time of year when the Goddess ruled supreme. The village morphed into fairyland of glowing oil lamps. Firecrackers illuminated the sky and the earth. The air was replete with ear splitting explosions; joyous screeches of children and the cry of vendors. Women paraded the street in their resplendent apparels and finery. Nattily dressed men proudly escorted their families. The season passed, the celebrations ended and a new Hindu year dawned. The Laxmi temple was swamped by visitors all through the holidays. He had collected enough money to make improvements on the shed. The villagers jokingly named the beggar Pundit.

Ever since he started to work in the school, Pundit had his heart set on Radhika. The girl also worked as a sweeper in the school. He would ply her with sweetmeats and cheap trinkets every pay day. She returned his attentions with shy smiles, giggles and flirtatious glances. But lack of finances stood in the way of wedded bliss. Over time, the temple's earnings increased manifold. Pundit enjoyed elevated social status. But Radhika remained diffident and shy. Pundit did not abandon hope. Every night he would lie in bed and plan clever ways to win her over. He would visit the school with his heart full of love poems and romantic songs. But when the time came to execute his plan, his voice and courage would fail him. Instead of wooing the love of his life with verse and song, he would stutter excuses to talk to her. However, she found his shyness endearing. He upgraded his gifts to silver trinkets. On auspicious occasions he would present her with gold trinkets. The first ones to catch on to his amorous advances were the students. They would hum a verse of some love song or pass witty remarks whenever Pundit passed by. In time Pundit gained confidence and Radhika lost her shyness. A romance blossomed. It was a simple wedding attended by her relatives and the schoolteacher. Two priests from the Vajeshwari temple performed the ceremony.

Tales of incredible miracles mushroomed in every quarter of society. The news spread like wild fire. The distraught and the devastated poured into Vajeshwari in droves. A journalist got wind of the statues magical powers. He printed an article of the miracles in a local newspaper. The reputation of the Goddess spread nationwide. The news was printed in every language paper all over India. Soon the rich joined the list of regular visitors. Donations beyond Pundit's wildest dreams poured in. Pundit erected a majestic temple on the outskirts of the village. About fifty yards away stood the hut of a highly respected old priest. The dome of the temple towered above every structure except the temple of the deity Vajeshwari. The humble fishnet that hid the statue from visitors was replaced with an elaborately embroidered lace curtain. A finely carved wooden dais stood in place of the crude mud platform. The edifice displayed intricate wooden carvings of various deities. As years went by Pundit was elected a member of the village elders. He was now rich, powerful and respected. He often boasted that nothing bad could happen to him. The Goddess had ensured him of that. But Radhika had misgivings. She sensed the powers of evil circling overhead. Her husband was straying dangerously away from the path of righteousness. It started with an occasional peg or two with his cronies. In time the occasional peg or two increased to several pegs a day. At times he would consume half a bottle on his own. Shakutala, the village vamp took advantage of his weakness and weaved her seductive charms on him. She was now his regular partner in bed. The vamp had commandeered most of his money. Radhika feared her husband was on his way to penury. Priests from the Vajeshwari temple and even the schoolmaster began to shun him. Pundit remained undeterred. He continued to believe that the Goddess would stand by him. Disturbing news reached Radhika through very reliable sources that Shakuntala was badgering Pundit to sell the statue. Under the influence of liquor and lust Pundit appeared to be weakening. He was overheard discussing the selling price of the statue with a wealthy visitor from Bombay. That night, Radhika and a number of priests from Vajeshwari temple transferred the statue to their temple. Pundit was beside himself with rage when he discovered that the statue was missing. They managed to convince the inebriated Pundit that the statue was stolen. Shakuntala showed her true colours. She refused to acknowledge Pundit's existence. A few days later Radhika found her husband hanging from a rafter of the temple. The Vajeshwari temple priests retransferred the statue back to the Laxmi temple. Shakuntala was hounded out of Vajeshwari. Radhika's faith in the Goddess did not ebb. The distraught widow of the late Pundit continued to spend all her time in dedicated service of the Goddess.

CHAPTER 23

Christopher Travers sat in his Bombay office looking older than his years. He appeared to have lost his zest for life. The theft of the statue and the death of his friends and staff continued to haunt him. He felt responsible for the tragedy. Most of all, he blamed himself for not having heeded the warning of the village priest. He should have waited for the skies to clear. Instead he foolishly trusted modern scientific knowledge over time tested beliefs. But the loss of the statue distressed him most of all.

Christopher employed Richard Morrison, a retired detective from Scotland Yard. Morrison and Harvey followed every lead to trace the statue. The two had made a number of trips to Vajeshwari since the theft. Every time they returned with nothing to show for their troubles. The thief and the statue had seemingly vanished from the surface of the earth. Morrison secretly believed that their efforts were in vain. However, he was not one to throw in the towel because of a few setbacks.

Christopher made one final visit to the village. He wished to reassure the villagers that he had not given up searching for their Goddess. Christopher, Harvey, Morrison and a missionary interpreter arrived at the village. His reception was subdued. The love and respect he had enjoyed in the past was discernibly missing. Much to his dismay, he found that the villager's attitudes towards religion had also changed. The younger generation of villagers shunned the rites and rituals of the past. It seemed the Goddess was not merely out of sight, she was also out of mind. The temple was merely a decaying ghost of its past splendour. The fields were dry and barren. The surrounding woods were evidently dying.

Christopher had hardly spoken a word since they returned. He felt his resolve to find the statue diminishing. Finally Morrison summoned the courage to opine that they were chasing a lost cause. Christopher decided to call off the search. Harvey and Morrison were relieved. Their meeting was interrupted by the entry of Christopher's secretary. She placed a newspaper on her boss's desk with the fervour of one who has discovered a lost treasure. She drew his attention to a column in the lower corner of the penultimate page. The brief essay told of a statue of the Goddess Lakshmi that granted wishes. It was rumoured that the statue was made of pure gold and precious stones. A man called Pundit who has devoted his life to the Goddess said her sudden appearance was nothing short of a miracle. But he stopped short of revealing any details. He sincerely believed she had chosen him to serve her. No matter how hard the journalists pressed him for more information, he refused to elaborate further on the matter. The article informed the reader that the Goddess is placed behind a lace curtain, hidden from the eyes of the rest of the world. No one, regardless of their social or official status, is granted permission to see the statue. The paper cited a list of examples of the Goddess's miracles. A long silence ensued. All three men were lost in their own thoughts. Harvey and Morrison remained sceptical. Harvey was the first to voice his opinion. He said that there was nothing in the article to suggest that this could be the same statue. He described the incidents cited as journalistic sensationalism. Christopher was in favour of revisiting the village. Morrison introduced a thought provoking note. He suggested that Christopher should use his influence to force the priest to unveil the statue for them. Christopher seconded Morrison's suggestion. Harvey was not convinced. Harvey's scepticism gave rise to an argument between Morrison and Harvey. Harvey opined that priests do not countenance authority when it comes to matters of religion. Christopher was adamant. He insisted they visit the temple. The boss's decision ended the argument once and for all.

The governor, the inspector general of police and the chief inspector of Vajeshwari were hesitant to permit him entry during the Diwali festivities. They warned of rowdy elements visiting the village. They did not have the necessary resources to control the crowds and ensure Christopher's safety at the same time.

CHAPTER 24

Liam Crowe was dismissed a month after the Howrah station debacle. He opted against returning to England. His reputation among the police fraternity lay in ruins. His family and friends in England were sure to shun him. Worst of all, his uncle would not miss an opportunity to shame him in the presence of his family and friends. Besides, his prospects of eking out an existence were far better here in India. Many years ago Singh had introduced him to Rungta, the infamous dealer in stolen artefacts. After his dismissal he renewed their old acquaintanceship. He scoured the country for antiques, jewellery and works of art. It did not matter if they were stolen or fake. In time he established contacts across the country. The deals helped keep hearth and home together. If he managed to get his hands on the statue, life would have been a different ball game. As it is, his earnings were at best average. He dreamed that someday, somewhere the grand prize was sure to surface. Whoever stole it must eventually put it up for sale in the grey market. He established contacts with underhanded dealers all over the world. At worst, he could alert the authorities and regain his lost reputation. He may even be reinstated in the force. Either way he would find himself in a win, win situation.

Crowe was surprised to receive an invitation from Rungta It came as a surprise as the dealer pointedly avoided calling agents. The invitation made him suspicious. Whatever the reason, he could not ignore a call from his main source of income. Finally he paid the dealer a visit.

Rungta ungraciously ordered Crowe to sit down. That was the be all and end all of the dealer's duty as a host. He asked Crowe to recall his final assignment as a police officer and his involvement with a statue. He asked if Crowe would recognise it, if he saw it again. Crowe was stunned to learn that the dealer knew of his past. He wondered what game the dealer was playing. If he answered in the negative, the dealer would dismiss him and search for someone else. Crowe took a gamble and uttered a hesitant croaky 'Yes'. Rungta handed him a newspaper clipping with the heading "Vajeshwari miracle statue". Rungta told him to visit Vajeshwari during the Diwali festival. His assignment was to find a way to see the miracle statue and inform him if the two were the same. He offered Crowe fifty thousand rupees plus expenses if he got hold of the statue. Considering the statue stood behind a veil, it would be a nearly impossible to see it. However Crowe agreed. There was the remote possibility of getting his hands on the artefact. He knew he was playing with fire. Rungta had the power and connections to have him eliminated with a click of a finger. He wished Singh were around. The blundering buffoon had a million faults. However, at times such as this the Sikh was indispensible.

CHAPTER 25

A junior cleric of a mosque in Bombay dreamed of converting the whole world to Islam. He laboured under the belief that Allah and the great prophet Mohamed had chosen him to lead mankind into an era of Islamic dominance. What began as a pipe dream had turned into a fixation. He would corner people and talk at length about it. Low ranking workers and helpers in the mosque did their best to avoid him. Some people humoured him, believing he was mentally disturbed. He declared Hindus, Christians, and Jews as the scum of humanity. The rest were insignificant. The three heathen races were formidable forces in their own rights. They were capable of offering the stiffest resistance. For them there would be no mercy. He would need to wipe them off the surface of the earth. He planned to achieve this by first creating religious conflicts between them. The religion that emerged victorious would face the wrath of his mighty Islamic army. The followers of the remaining faiths would be given the option to convert or die. Their numbers were insignificant. Either way, they would pose little or no problem. In the service of Allah, Mohamed and Islam anything was permissible. He believed that ethnic cleansing would be unfortunate but necessary. The blame for the executions would lie squarely on the shoulders of those who refused conversion. The maniacal cleric spent many hours dreaming of the day his self-imposed service to Islam would dawn. To achieve his goal he needed large sums of money. One did not find a large army of professionally trained men in a lucky dip. He would also need an army of clerics to spread the word of prophet Mohamed throughout the world. So far everyone he approached rejected his scheme and branded him as insane. They called it an unrealistic fantasy of an immature mind. In time they would pay for their audacity. They would all be annihilated and their wealth transferred to womb. He regarded them as his future bankers. He would need to transfer the headquarters out of this country. India was unsuitable to realise his dreams. It was predominantly a Hindu stronghold. Worse, it was governed by the ever meddling British who followed the teachings of Jesus Christ. The two heathen sects could foil his plans before it took off. Most of Asia and Africa was also infested with British influence. On a Haj to Mecca, he had approached the royal family of Saudi Arabia to finance his grand scheme. They unceremoniously threw him out of the royal palace. It was a slap in the face. They would come to regret it when he ruled the world. Undeterred, he decided to go it alone.

Time rolled by. The cleric was getting desperate. One morning, while reading an Urdu newspaper, his eye fell on an article that aroused his interest. The article reported of a priceless statue of a Hindu Goddess in the village of Vajeshwari. The article claimed that the statue performed miracles. The Urdu newspaper ridiculed the claims. He agreed with them. Miracles could only be performed by Allah and the prophet. The article described the statue as one made of gold adorned with priceless precious stones. The article averred that it was in probability a rumour. However the description roused his curiosity. 'Damn the miracles' the cleric muttered. He calculated that if the description was anywhere near accurate, that statue would be worth millions. The cleric decided that the proof of the pudding was in the tasting of it. The tasting would entail taking a look. But he was a Moslem. If he was found anywhere near that statue it would be the end of him and his dreams. What he needed was an ally of Hindu origin. That would not be difficult to find. He knew of scores of Hindus willing to do his bidding for a price. Firstly he would retain one or two Hindus to sneak a peek. If they reported a gold statue truly existed, he would make preparations to storm the temple and steal it. With millions under his belt, he would be well on his way to realising his ultimate dream. The founders of Womb could go suck eggs. A few days later his luck changed. A highly influential imam in Lahore dubbed the evil imam, wished to learn the truth about the press reports. He chose the cleric to do the needful. The evil imam sent six strongmen to accompany the cleric. They travelled to Vajeshwari in a local train.

CHAPTER 26

The village of Vajeshwari is nestled in the heart of a densely wooded area on the outskirts of Bombay. Besides the temple of the local Deity Vajeshwari, the other attraction of the village is a spa said to possess healing powers. The two attractions combined drew a number of visitors of every strata of society. Each year a fair was held there in the deity's honour. For the entire week the fair was in progress, the village was overrun with thousands of visitors. As the event coincided with Diwali, the organisers expected record numbers to descend on the village.

Bassien railway station bore the burden of the hordes visiting Vajeshwari. Crowe stepped out of the station and decided to engage a taxi. His trip was paid for by Rungta, so he might as well travel in luxury. They branched off the western highway onto a single carriage road bordered by paddy fields. The taxi was forced to stop at the outskirts of the village. The throng made progress impossible. As he had no luggage, Crowe disengaged the cab and decided to join the crowd. The sheer force of people carried him onwards. They moved toward the temple of the deity Vajeshwari. One needed to climb a steep flight of steps to reach the temple. No guard railings marked the outer edges of the stairs. The exposed sides made Crowe nervous and a bit dizzy. He was fearful of being thrown over the side. Trusting in the powers of the deity, the followers ascended the steps without a concern. They believed that visitors either trusted the deity or refrained from visiting the temple. Crowe was an unbeliever who was here for a wicked purpose. He elbowed his way closer to the centre of the flight of steps.

The steps led to a large open area crammed to bursting point with worshipers. Colourful petals and leaves were strewn across the tiled floor. Statues of the three holy sisters sat under an awning in a cordoned off area. They appeared to welcome the devotees. Priests recited verses from Holy Scriptures. Small hand held symbols accompanied the rhythmic chanting. The deep resonance of large bells punctuated the recitation. Women lent an air of gaiety with their brilliantly coloured apparel. Children added to the festive mood with their senseless giggles and aimless games. A number of men in saffron robes and anointed foreheads minded the crowds. Worshipers displayed varying ways of showing respect. The old and infirm merely stood with folded hands and bowed heads. Some worshipers knelt before the deity. The overzealous devotees lay flat on their bellies before the altar. The throng was instructed to circle the altar in a clockwise direction once they paid their respects. The ritual ensured the blessings of the deity and her sisters. Crowe joined his hands, bowed his head and sleepwalked his way around the altar. He stood on the top of the stairs and viewed the steep descent with trepidation. It seemed he was looking down at the world from Mount Everest. It had a profound effect on his nervous system. He descended one careful step after another. Preoccupied with his descent, he found himself just an arm's length away from the edge of the steps. The sheer drop made him weak in the knees. His limbs trembled, his pulse raced, his head spun and his heart beat fast and furious. Overcome by vertigo, he was forced to stop. It infuriated the crowd. Crowe answered with a look of apology.

After what seemed an unending walk with death, Crowe managed to reach terra firma in one piece. He exhaled a deep breath of relief. He wondered what compelled people to risk life and limb just to go around three statues. Crowe was carried by the crowd towards an unknown destination. He wondered where they were heading. He hesitated to ask specifically for the location of the miracle temple. The temple was after all, one that functioned under the veil of secrecy. After all, Englishmen were known to ridicule their religion. He casually asked a man if there were any other temples worth visiting. The man informed him that they were headed for the temple of Goddess Laxmi. Crowe could barely contain his joy. On the way, he noticed a number of men from the Muslim community enjoying the funfair. It was a surprising contradiction to the norms and beliefs of both faiths. In Islam persons from other castes were considered heathens and infidels. To pay homage to a Hindu deity was considered sacrilege. The crowd arrived at the outer gate of the miracle temple. It was situated on the outskirts of the village. The temple was surrounded by thick woods. A small thatched hut behind it was the only other structure in the vicinity. The authorities divided the visitors in two orderly lines, one for women and children and the other for men. Every five minutes the line would move ten paces. He doubted he would get a chance before tea time. He was getting restless and irritable. The sun beat down bright and hot on his white shark's skin suit. He felt he was being cooked alive. The thought of a broiled Englishman in a strictly vegetarian temple amused him. Just before tea time the priests shut the temple gates. Those unwilling to relinquish their place waited in the queue, while others drifted off for some tea, snacks and a smoke. Crowe decided to stay put. The quicker he completed his mission, the quicker he could head home.

Crowe entered the holy sanctum well past teatime. Burning oil lamps and colourful garlands lent some relief to the drab visitor's hall. He noticed a richly embroidered lace curtain. Crowe's heart beat wildly. He was but a few yards from the treasure that could change his life. He constantly bent his head in the hope of getting a glimpse of the statue. He searched for a place where he could hide after the hall was closed. A young priest ushered him and a few others towards the lace veil. They were then led through a back room to the rear entrance. He stepped out of the temple into the evening light and stopped to consider his next move. Suddenly a familiar face stepped through the crowd. Rungta stood before him like an army general, inspecting a wayward soldier. The two men greeted each other in contrasting styles. Rungta's voice echoed strict business, while Crowe stuttered in shock and amazement. Rungta led him away from the temple towards the northern edge of the woods. 'What brings you here?' Crowe asked, confounded by Rungta's unexpected presence. Rungta avoided answering the question. Crowe believed the dealer was up to tricks. The suspected that he crafty dealer was looking for ways to double cross him. Rungta questioned Crowe about the statue. Crowe fixed on the dealer a look of incredulity. 'I do not possess ex-ray vision? How in God's name could I possibly know if it is the same statue?'

CHAPTER 27

After Pundit passed away, the priest of the Vajeshwari temple instructed Radhika in the complexities of running a temple. Radhika was now the sole caretaker. The priest supervised the preparations for the oncoming festivities. He found Radhika to be distracted. She went about her business in a trancelike state. It worried the Vajeshwari priest. When he questioned her, she was initially reticent, but relented under the priest's persistent badgering. She admitted that she was plagued by the feeling of some imminent catastrophe. The priest was a believer in premonitions and intuitions. He immersed himself in deep meditation. 'We must shift the Goddess to the old priest's hut. It should be safe there. But it must be done after sunset. Prying eyes are everywhere.' The priest's words sent a chill down Radhika's spine.

The hut was the residence of an old retired priest from the Vajeshwari temple. He still commanded obedience and respect from one and all. Since his retirement he had sworn off all worldly pleasures. His intake of food was meagre and sparse. He lived a quiet contented life in his humble abode. Apart from junior priests, his regular visitors were rats, geckos, scorpions, snakes and feral dogs. The canines would poke their heads through the doorway in the hope of a hand out. Though a strict vegetarian, he kept bits of meat for his four legged guests. A female leopard often paid a visit. She sat a short distance away from the hut, as if guarding the man of God. Miraculously the priest was never harmed by any of his mammalian, reptilian or insect visitors. An unexpected visit from the head priest of

Vajeshwari temple came as a welcome surprise. The old priest noticed the look of anguish on his visitors face.

'It seems there are evil forces at work all around us' the head priest said apprehensively.

'But that has been true since the dawn of time. We must keep faith in the creator and carry on.'

The young head priest told him of Radhika's intuition and his doubts and fears. The old priest sat unmoved. 'Whatever happens will only happen if the Goddess wills it so.'

'I plan on transferring the statue to your hut. But I fear that could jeopardise your life.'

'Young man, death is an integral part of all existence. Galaxies, solar systems, stars and planets must die to make way for the next generation. Mountains erode and seas and rivers run dry. That has been the scheme of things since the dawn of time. More importantly, interference with life and death is an encumbrance to karma. And karma is solely the domain of the Almighty. If I must die so be it. I am eighty seven years old. How much longer do you expect me to go on? As for the statue, it has a preordained destiny to fulfil. It will soon leave us, and no one can prevent it.' The prediction, that neither the old priest nor the miracle Goddess will be with them for long, left the Vajeshwari priest in a state of deep depression.

****

The Vajeshwari police were stretched to breaking point. The chief reeled under the pressure of managing rowdy crowds and unscrupulous criminals. Moreover, he was burdened with the task of protecting Christopher and company. He could not ignore orders from the governor. They were secretly whisked away to a government guest house. Only a handful of policemen were aware of their presence. He also faced the arduous task of convincing the head priest and Radhika to permit Christopher to see the statue. At first Radhika remained circumspect. But after numerous assurances from the chief, she reluctantly agreed. However, both the priest and Radhika stipulated that neither he nor Harvey and Morrison would be permitted near the statue. Around midnight, they drove Christopher to the old priest's hut.

CHAPTER 28

In the northern section of the woods, Rungta and Crowe had a long and exhaustive discussion. He regarded Rungta's plan to steal the statue as foolhardy. The dealer had recruited a gang of hoodlums to raid the temple. Hoodlums as a rule were violent and undisciplined. The religious guardians of the statue may be simple villagers, but they were not fools. A religious artefact of such immense religious value would not remain unguarded for a single moment. They were keenly aware of the hordes of strangers visiting the temple every day. Rungta could face the wrath of millions of devotees. Crowe gauged Rungta to be an astute dealer but a damn fool tactician. Crowe knew from experience that unforeseen events do ruin the best of plans. In his opinion, the dealer was leading his hoodlums into the jaws of death. Rungta suggested that Crowe should return to Bombay, on the first available train and await his arrival. Crowe decided to ignore the advice. Once the statue was in Rungta's hands, there was no telling if he would keep his end of the bargain. More so, there was the off chance that he could get his hands on it before the dealer. He decided to hang around and watch from a distance. He knew he would have just one chance. He had to make the most of it. The temple officials ushered the last batch of devotees out of the rear entrance and locked all the doors and gates. Crowe waited till the last of the worshipers had left. The shadows lengthened, seeping the temple and its surroundings in darkness. Crowe surveyed the area from a distance. For the first time he noticed the hut behind the temple. Its presence worried him. The hut could be a temporary police outpost.

Crowe spotted movement at the rear entrance of the temple. Four silhouettes grappled with something heavy. It aroused his curiosity. He watched the shadows carry the heavy article from the temple to the hut. He thought long and hard about the strange occurrence. After sunset, villagers generally confine themselves to their homes and priests are busy with temple duties. They do not spend their time lugging heavy loads like coolies at a railway station. Crowe suspected that they were either involved in some nefarious activity or some secret mission. He concluded that their strange activity had something to do with the statue. The thought that Rungta would raid the temple and find the statue missing made him chuckle. He realised he was the only person other than the moving shadows who knew of the new location of the statue. He scoffed at Rungta's offer of fifty thousand. If things went his way, the statue could be his for the taking. The operation involved a lot of risks but the rewards would be worth it.

Crowe had seen all he needed to see. He decided to return to the village. The main road was a good bit brighter. The kerosene lamps on fast food trolleys dissipated the darkness. Unpleasant kerosene fumes permeated the air. Groups of rowdy revellers lingered around the stalls. They laughed raucously and shouted ribald remarks at each other. He noticed that a group of devout worshipers, waited patiently for the last bus. The rowdy elements walked past without paying him any heed. Some of them were Muslims. Their presence continued to baffle him. It was like seeing Jews in Mecca during the Id pilgrimage. Curiously, their presence seemed to be accepted by the Hindus. He searched for logical explanations. Most of the Muslims were in their teens or early twenties. Their bachelor status explained the absence of women and children. Maybe they were here to enjoy the attractions of the fair. Maybe this particular lot were converts. A chilling thought entered his mind. He slapped his forehead and chided himself not having guessed it right away. The article in the newspaper had brought them here. It must have been read by thousands of Muslims. The avaricious must have aspired to purloin the statue. That was it, he concluded. Things were getting interesting. His chances of stealing the statue increased. All hell would break lose when Rungta's hoodlums, the Muslim marauders met at the temple. All he needed to do was patiently wait for an opportune moment and strike when the iron was hot.

Crowe treated himself to tea and snacks. The rowdy youngsters drifted away into the night. The echoes of their songs and laughter gradually faded away. The vendors shut shop. The village main road stood as dark, still and silent as the woods around the temple. Crowe was tempted to rent a comfortable room in a hotel. He decided against it. It had been a long day. He feared he may fall asleep. It was crucial for him to stay awake. He needed to be at the right place at the right time. A lost opportunity was unacceptable. He found a secluded spot on the side of the road and parked his weary body on a large rock and waited for events to unfold. His wait was far from peaceful. A myriad of tiny and not so tiny dive bombers targeted his face and hands. An army of creepy crawlies took a fancy to him. Some decided to crawl up his trouser. He suffered it all in silence. Around midnight, an official car sped past. It headed towards the temple. Crowe grew anxious. He believed something must have a happened to make officials race there in the dead of night.

CHAPTER 29

Christopher entered the old priest's hut alone. The head priest of the Vajeshwari temple and Radhika were already there. He was warmly welcomed by the old priest. To everyone's surprise, the old priest spoke fluent English. Christopher steered the conversation from small talk to the matter at hand. At the old priest's request, Christopher narrated in detail the history of the statue. The only time old priest displayed any emotion was when Christopher mentioned the murders. The tragic tale immersed the old priest in deep thought. He revealed his guru had predicted he would witness Goddess Laxmi's power at the time of his final days on earth. Being young and naïve he forgot all about it. When Pundit returned to the village, the prediction came flooding back.

The old priest's tale was received differently by those in the hut. Christopher, who had been told of the mysterious wonders of India by his mother, kept an open mind. Radhika wondered if the old priest was trying to convey a message. Or, was he merely trying to entertain them with an interesting anecdote? The Vajeshwari temple priest sat frozen with fear. The old priest led Christopher through a secret door at the far corner of the hut. The existence of the door surprised him. He had been facing it without realising it existed. The room was no bigger than a walk in closet. The old priest handed Christopher his precious statue but advised him to leave the statue in the hut. 'I understand that you are emotionally attached to the statue. But the statue possesses the spirit of the Goddess. It has been assigned a mission that it must fulfil. He warned against interfering with the

Goddess's plans. The old priest foretold that many would die in pursuit of the statue. Before they left, he requested the chief of police not to have his men stationed round the temple. It would only cause more bloodshed.

CHAPTER 30

Crowe fought off the effects of drowsiness, heaved himself to his feet and made his way towards the temple. He felt stiff and sore. Soon he was walking at a brisk pace. When he reached the temple, he found the area still and silent. He noticed a police car parked outside the hut. Three men stood by the car. A pack of stray dogs occupied the plot between the temple and the hut. The dogs eyed him with suspicion. They growled and barked. He feared their barking might alert those around. He retraced his steps and waited for events to unfold.

Crowe approached the temple cautiously. He scaled the low picket fence and made his way to the front door. His eyes and ears were alert to the merest sound and movement. Crowe noticed that the lock was worn and rusty. The lock gave way with a single blow from a stone. The absence of priests and policemen made him bolder. He crept in and stopped just inside the doorway. He searched for signs of occupancy. He was prepared to flee at the first hint of an approaching human. The dim glow of two oil lamps struggled to illuminate the length and breadth of the hall. The lace curtain seemed to beacon him. Just as he expected, the niche was empty. He wondered if those shadows were priests or thieves. There was no sense wasting time in the temple. He transferred his attention to the hut.

He recalled the rear entrance of the temple. He tiptoed across the small rear room. He undid the brass stopper and silently opened the backdoor wide enough to give him a view of the hut. The car and the three men were still there. An oil lamp illuminated the single window of the hut. Crowe decided to wait and watch further developments. Finally, a man stepped out of the hut and the car drove away with the three silhouettes.

Sounds of activity at the temple's front door fell on Crowe's ears. He hurried out of the rear entrance and carefully made his way across the open plot. The dogs eyed him with suspicion. The crunch of loose gravel added to his discomfort. Crowe sat crouched behind a bush and speculated on the purpose of the hut. If a policeman exited the hut, he would high tail it back to Bombay. It would be a major blow to his livelihood. His attention was drawn to a shadowy figure stepping out of the hut. The mysterious individual was a pint sized man who clicked his fingers to call his canine companions. In a matter of seconds, the pack circled him, wildly wagging their tails. After feeding the mutts, the pint sized man retreated into the hut.

****

Rungta and his hoodlums approached the temple through the woods. They prepared to raid the temple. The sight of the unguarded temple emboldened him. However, presence of stray dogs was source of worry. Those mongrels were capable of waking heaven and hell at the mere sight of strangers. Rungta paid little heed to the hut. He believed it was the residence of some poor villager. The car outside the hut stopped them in their strides. Finally a man emerged from the hut and the car sped away. Using the trees as cover, they silently made their way to the temple. Two men helped Rungta climb over the picket fence. The broken lock and the open door made him suspicious. He wondered if someone had beaten him to the post. Rungta warily stepped into the temple and peered through the semi-darkness. He took his time to ensure that no one was around. He tiptoed his way towards the veiled niche. The dying flames of some of the oil lamps flickered, casting eerie shadows. He could barely wait for the moment the grand prize was in his grasp. He felt like Attila the Hun, about to commandeer the spoils of war. He drew the lace curtain with the dramatic fervour of Dorian Grey unfurling his portrait. His jaw dropped, his body froze and his brain went numb. He stood transfixed, staring at the empty niche, with only a flickering flame staring back at him. He uttered the name Crowe between clenched teeth. His attention was drawn to the archway that led to the back room. To his relief he found he was alone. A loud bang made him skip like a frisky kangaroo. He risked lighting his torch. The breeze had caused the rear door to slam. He was forced to hurdle over a number of obstacles to reach it. Rungta saw a lone figure enter the hut. He was convinced the lone figure was Crowe. He had to catch up with the double crosser before he disappeared into the woods. Rungta knew that once Crowe arrived in Bombay the chances of catching him were slim. Rungta decide to follow the mysterious shadow into the hut.

****

The sun dipped over the horizon. He could barely contain his enthusiasm. The cleric decided it was time into put his plan in action. He could barely wait for the moment he would hold the statue in his arms. In the company of his muscle bound bodyguards made their way to the temple. It appeared eerily forbidding in the darkness. He reminded himself that a Hindu temple should not intimidate a Muslim. The cleric stepped into the temple alone. He worried that the sight of the statue might kindle the greed of the others. The still and silent congregation hall sent a chill up his spine. He thought he saw the silhouettes of a host of Hindu deities staring down at him. Mouthing the word Allah under his breath, he inched towards the lace veil. He lifted it gently with trembling hands. For a brief moment he stood nonplussed, staring uncomprehendingly at the empty niche. He pondered over the nasty trick fate had played on him. He was at a loss to understand why Allah had permitted such deception. It gradually dawned on him that it wasn't Allah but the Goddess who had put a spoke in the wheel. She was not prepared to let a Muslim take possession of the statue. The sound of movement from somewhere behind the temple urged him to retrace his steps. The cleric stepped out of the temple a broken man.

The cleric decided not to let a Hindu Goddess thwart his plan. This time he entered the temple with his entire force in tow. He had about him the air of Julius Caesar marching towards one of his many conquests. He recalled the sound of movement he had heard earlier. He ordered his men to survey the open plot. 'Kill the bastard if necessary' he ordered. He wanted no witnesses when he carried away the statue in his large shoulder bag. When he returned to the mosque, he would stash it away in some secret location. To make his plan fool proof, he would need to find a way to kill all his companions. They returned with the news that no one was there.

The cleric knew he had not imagined the sound he had heard. They made their way through the rear room and onto the open plot. The thought of facing failure and humiliation urged him on. A pack of barking dogs waited to greet him. He spotted a man enter the hut. Throwing caution to the wind, he decided to follow.

****

From his hideout, Crowe watched the pack of dogs wander away from the hut. The presence of the pint sized man in the hut made him wary. The man's congeniality with the mutts added to his discomfort. Dogs were reputed to be fiercely loyal. Cautiously he inched his way towards the hut. He waited apprehensively by the entrance before stepping in. He stood motionless, surveying the dim interior. A single oil lamp illuminated a crudely made altar. The rest of the room remained in total darkness. He hesitatingly switched on his torch. He saw a brass kerosene stove and some utensils in one corner. A wooden chest stood at the other end. Crowe proceeded to inspect inner part of the hut. A slightly built old man blocked his way. 'What you seek will be the cause of your death' the old man croaked. 'The Goddess has predetermined the statue's fate. Beware her wrath.'

'If you don't relinquish the statue, I will be the cause of your death' Crowe responded threateningly.

The priest did not respond. He led the intruder into a small room. The statue stood in a corner, glaring at Crowe. Crowe decided to kill the old priest. Before he could seize the old priest's throat, he heard someone enter the hut. The priest quickly extinguished the oil lamp.

****

Rungta was not one to accept defeat easily. He had not made his millions by surrendering to setbacks. He calculated that even if the description of the statue was fifty per cent accurate, it would be worth millions. Such a priceless artefact was not meant to be in a temple, worshiped by simpletons. It should be part of a collection of someone who could truly appreciate it. Crowe was nothing more than a cheap crook.

Rungta scanned the plot between the temple and the hut. Not a soul was in sight. Even the pack of mongrels had abandoned the area. He noticed a jigsaw puzzle of footprints outside the hut. He concluded that they belonged to the recent visitors. One particular set of freshly made imprints caught his attention. Rungta was certain they belonged to Crowe. He silently entered the hut alone. He waited at the entrance with pistol in hand, listening for sound of movement. His heart beat like an excavator's drill and his pulse raced out of control. The absence of any sound ensured him the hut was unoccupied. But that was not entirely good news. The wily fox may have fled into the woods from a rear entrance. Rungta inched his way into the room. The rasping sound of heavy breathing fell on his ears. Rungta was elated. Crowe was still inside the hut. Rungta crept towards the sound. Gradually the rasping grew louder. Suddenly a door flew open. It was followed by a deafening explosion. The deafening sound reverberated in the confines of the hut. Rungta felt the rush of air as a bullet whizzed past his face. He returned fire. His target flew several feet back and disappeared into the dark alcove. Shaken to the core, Rungta lit his torch with trembling hands. The sight of Crowe with blood gushing out of his chest gladdened his heart. Suddenly a prune like face appeared out of the shadows. The two locked eyes for a brief moment. The man wore the garb of a priest. The priest was clasping a bundle close to his chest, with the fervour of an over protective mother. Rungta was well aware of the blind illogical faith of Hindu priests. He was left with no option but to shoot the intrepid old man. The old priest fell to the floor, still clasping the precious bundle to his chest. He bent to wrench the bundle from the dead priest's grasp, when he sensed a presence behind him. He turned as quickly as he could. Rungta felt a volley of four bullets enter his body. One of the bullets shattered his spine. A fountain of blood sprayed the walls. The dealer of stolen artefacts lay dead on the dung carpeted floor, with his sightless eyes wide open.

****

The cleric nervously entered the hut. His torch beam illuminated the doorway to a small room. He saw a man stooped over a dead body. The man spun around with a gun in his hand. In a state of panic he blindly fired four shots. The man lay there motionless. Something glimmered in the beam of his torch. He lifted the statue and looked heavenwards. 'Praised be Allah' he muttered. The cleric and his men made their way back to the woods. The cleric retreated behind a clump of bushes. He reloaded his gun and opened fire. All the evil imam's strongmen lay dead on the dewy earth.

CHAPTER 31

The cleric returned to the village. Policemen were everywhere. A check post was erected on the road to Bassein. They checked every vehicle leaving the village. The cleric shared a cab with three old men. He slipped into the centre of the rear seat. The taxi stopped at the check point. A policeman took a long look at the passengers. The cleric's nerves were close to breaking point. He hoped his frail physique, sunken cheeks and ashen pallor might deceive the cop. After a long tense moment the cab was flagged through.

The cleric arrived at his mosque in Bombay fatigued and dishevelled. He managed to sneak into his room unnoticed. He hid the bundle in a safe place and drifted into the dreamless. Around teatime he heard a knocking on his chamber door. The cleric's mood was that of a grumpy grizzly bear. The messenger stuttered that the imam had wished to see him and departed as fast as his legs could carry him.

The cleric wanted to ignore the order but decided against it. The local imam was a kind and gentle person but possessed zero tolerance for insubordination. The cleric nearly jumped out of his skin when he saw Rafiq Ali Khan in the imam's chamber. Khan was the head honcho of Womb. He harboured a deep dislike for the cleric. On several occasions he aired the opinion that the cleric should have chosen a career as a clown. The cleric fought against his fears. He reasoned that there was no reason to fret. Khan could not possibly know what had transpired at Vajeshwari. Khan wasted no time to come to the reason for his visit. 'I believe you are in possession of a statue' Khan said. The statement gave the cleric quite a jolt. He categorically denied it.

He rattled off a fabricated tale of how some other gang had beaten him to it. 'So where are the rest of the imam's men from Lahore?' Khan noticed the cleric's discomfort and decided put the man under more pressure. 'I want a detailed account of your encounter with the other gang' Khan urged. The cleric started to squirm and fidget. 'There is very little to tell' he stuttered. 'The gang was larger and better armed than we were. They slaughtered our men like sheep in an abattoir. By the grace of Allah I managed to escape.'

'Did you see the statue?'

'No, it was veiled.'

The imam quickly caught on to the cleric's subterfuge. He recalled the cleric telling him that the men were killed in a police encounter. He dismissed the cleric like a lowly serf. In the cleric's absence, the imam assured Khan he would have the statue in his possession in a day or two. The Bombay imam received a telegram from the evil imam of Lahore, ordering that the cleric and the statue be sent to Lahore on the first available train. They must be accompanied by his strongmen.

The cleric was eager to go to Lahore. He feared the astute Bombay police would soon arrest him. He planned to escape en route to Lahore. He would surely find a buyer. With the millions he would launch his own Womb. Khan would be his first victim. The cleric left Bombay in the company of Rahim, Khan's right hand man. He alone was more intimidating than all of the evil imam's men. He was not someone to be messed with.

****

The cleric arrived in Lahore, apprehensive to face the evil imam. The man's reputation preceded him. The cleric decided to be humble and subservient. Hardly had he settled in, when he received a summons. The imam's attitude was brusque and dictatorial. 'I don't want to see you I want to see the statue.'

When the cleric presented statue the imam's joy was plainly visible. He sat staring wide eyed, at the artefact. 'This is more than a king's ransom' he muttered to himself. 'You have done well.'

The atmosphere of joy and bonhomie was marred by the unexpected entry of Rafiq Ali Khan. The cleric and the evil imam stared in utter surprise. Khan's visits to the city were usually heralded well in advance. Khan too was overwhelmed by the sight of the statue. He was a connoisseur and an avid collector of rare artefacts. But he had to admit he had never seen anything like it before. Khan could sense the discomfort. However, he had not come to Lahore to win a popularity contest. He glared fixedly at the cleric until the man got the message and left the room. 'If I find you with your ear to the door, I will deal extremely harshly with you' Khan warned.

'What brings you to Lahore?' the imam asked when they were alone.

'What do you think?' Khan replied, fixing his eyes on the statue.

The evil imam displayed discomfort. He sensed they were heading for a confrontation. 'Well, here it is and here it will stay' the imam said, emphatically.

Khan took a moment to martial his thoughts. 'How well do you know the cleric?' he asked.

'Well enough to select him to accomplish a risky mission.'

'Of all people, why did you choose him?

'I needed a scapegoat if things went wrong. The fool is dispensable. My men were instructed to eliminate him once they retrieved the statue. But Allah had different ideas. Both you and I know that no one disposes what Allah proposes. So here we are, saddled with a liability.'

'That man is not just a liability he is a danger to Womb. For some time he has been entertaining the belief that Allah has chosen him to head the Islamic community. He has told everyone who cared to listen that he is waiting for adequate finance. That statue will provide more finance than he seeks. In short, the statue is not safe as long as the cleric and the statue remain in the mosque at the same time.'

The imam coughed out a snigger. 'I am more than capable of taking care of my assets.'

'You will store it in that safe behind your desk. Take my word for it that safe is not thief proof.'

'That safe is as secure as a bank vault.'

Khan had no option but to be blunt. 'Not as long as the cleric is around' he replied, I wouldn't put it past him to find an opportunity to make a copy of the keys.'

The imam took a moment to quell his rising anger. Khan had managed to shake the imam's self-confidence. For a space of time the evil imam sat silent and thoughtful. The statue was an irreplaceable asset.

'Very well, I'll deposit it in the mosque's bank.'

'We need two signatures to operate that vault. What if I am not around when you need it?'

Khan had put a spoke in the evil imam's devious plan. He half-heartedly handed over the statue to Khan. Long after Khan left, the imam brooded over the unforeseen developments.

The cleric watched with dismay as Khan carried the statue away. He rushed into the imam's room to urge the religious chief to stop Khan before it was too late. The imam glared at the cleric with the intensity of an irate tiger. He was fed up of people barging in and out of his room without prior permission. 'Step out, close the door, knock and enter when I tell you.' It was evident that the mood of the imam had changed for the worse. The cleric did as he was told like an obedient schoolboy. He questioned the cleric regarding his obsession about the statue.

'You have made a terrible mistake. You will never see the statue again unless you act now. Khan does not part with expensive artefacts once he gets his hands on them.'

The imam gathered his thoughts before answering. 'In any conflict, whether it is between two individuals or two armies, there is an aspect called strategic retreat. Khan made several very compelling arguments. Had I not heeded the arguments, Khan would have gone away, believing I was attempting to keep the statue for myself. That would have caused more friction between us. Womb can do without internal conflict right now. Trust me, when the time is right, I will wrest the statue from him by hook or crook. Now kindly leave me alone.'

CHAPTER 32

The life of the chief inspector of Vajeshwari was at an all-time low. The public and his seniors blamed him for not safeguarding the statue. They also blamed him for not protecting the old priest. His reputation in the force had taken a severe blow. His wife was diagnosed with cancer. The cost of the treatment had seeped him deep in debt. A shady character named Rungta had offered him a hundred thousand rupees to look the other way when he stole the statue. To prove his bona fides, the dealer had given him twenty five thousand in advance. Under the circumstances, it was an offer he could not refuse. However, he had planned to arrest the dealer and reinstate the statue in the temple when the opportunity presented itself. But things did not go according to plan. The damn fool dealer had himself killed. The statue was gone. There was no way of knowing the identity of the perpetrator. The chief suspected it was one of the dealer's men, but that was mere speculation. He was determined to bring the criminals to justice, even if it was the last thing he did.

The chief inspector informed Christopher of the theft. He noticed a look of anguish wash over the millionaire's face. Harvey and Morrison were pained by the look of despair on their boss's face. They offered to assist the chief inspector in the investigation. The two men raced to the temple with the chief. Christopher was left in the guest house, protected by armed policemen.

The front room of the old priest's hut appeared untouched. However, the small room resembled a block of dark brown Swiss cheese. It was pockmarked with innumerable bullet holes.

Harvey and Morrison thoroughly inspected the hut. The nauseating stench of blood permeated the confined area. Morrison observed there were no signs of a struggle. He suspected the involvement of a third man who was probably in possession of the statue. When they stepped out of the hut, Morrison pointed to the imprint of a shoe worn mainly by Muslim men. The chief inspector was clearly embarrassed. He should not have missed seeing the foot print. They turned their attention to the temple. The temple had escaped the onslaught of the marauding factions. Besides the torn curtain and a few footprints, the temple stood proud and unharmed. A junior priest led them to the ante room. Morrison noticed a number of different footprints in the dust. He could tell they were made at different times. One of them was identical to the print of the Muslim shoe outside the hut. Morrison, Harvey, the chief and a handful of junior policemen followed the Muslim shoe prints into the forest. They came upon a forest clearing where several bodies lay dead. They widened the search area. Harvey's eyes fell on a thicket that appeared recently disturbed. He found a bag. In it they found a Koran with the name and address of a mosque in Bombay and an automatic handgun. A heated argument broke out between Morrison and the chief. Both men wanted to take possession of the gun and the Koran. Harvey suggested they take the gun to the chief justice and let him decide. The chief relented. He had no inclination to face chief justices while his professional reputation was on the line.

Christopher, Harvey, Morrison and the chief drove to the morgue in Bassien. Harvey instantly recognised Crowe. The retired S.A.S. officer shook with rage and hate. 'That is the unscrupulous bastard. I had a feeling all along that he would be involved in something like this. Since the time of Mister Travers' accident I have distrusted that man. I would not be the least bit surprised if he turned out to be the mastermind behind the theft.'

On their return journey Morrison and Harvey discussed the investigation. Christopher sat crestfallen, lost in deep contemplation. He was inclined to end the investigation.

BOOK 2

Continued on page 215

CHAPTER 1

Soon after his parents were murdered in the temple, reverend Beech took Gautam, the murdered priest's son under his care. He was only seven years old at the time. As time went by, the child felt quite at home in the hospital. All the priests and staff of the hospital pampered him. Reverend Beech oversaw every aspect of Gautam's education. Though he too indulged the child, he was firm when he needed to be. He taught the boy to speak, read and write English, learn basic maths, study world history and geography. For six years Gautam's life was a bed of roses. However, time and again that dreadful night would return to haunt him. Every sound and smell remained clearly etched in his mind. It still sent a chill down his spine. He recalled lying next to his mother. He could still feel her comforting warmth. The various sounds of the jungle rang in his head. While his father made preparations for the evening prayers and his mother prepared dinner, he played imaginary games. That fateful night, his father cut short his preparations and rushed into the storeroom and warned them to remain in the storeroom. It was all very confusing. His father had never taken time off from his duties. Their curiosity was too strong to ignore. His mother and he crept to the storeroom door. An alien creature with pale colourless skin; hay coloured hair and the dimensions of a monster had entered Goddess's sanctum. His father kept the monster at bay with the business end of a trident. The two men circled each other. He watched the fight with admiration and pride. His father was giving the monster a run for his money. But suddenly things went horribly wrong. He watched the monster plunge the trident into his father's chest. He could still hear his father's dying groan. The sight paralysed him with terror. Without warning, his mother charged at the monster, screaming like an unhinged woman. She grappled with the creature, wildly kicking and clawing him. She was no match for the fiendish giant. However, she fought free of his clutches and ran out of the chamber. In a blink of an eye she disappeared out of sight. He saw the monster run after her. He had no idea of her fate until he returned with the villagers. Among the mess that littered the chamber floor, they found a wallet. It contained ninety seven rupees and a calling card. Reverend Beech informed them that the card belonged to Christopher Travers. It had his Bombay address on it. The villagers could scarcely believe their ears. It was after the reverend related the unfortunate incident on the hill, that everyone's anger was allayed. The following day both his parents were cremated. The villagers urged the reverend to take Gautam under his wing.

Now the time had come to part with the man he considered his second father. The church had summoned the reverend back to Rome. The news left him depressed and disturbed. The reverend attempted to dispel his fears with encouraging words like 'Always remember that you are never truly alone. God, Jesus and the Goddess will always be with you in light or darkness.' But that did little to dispel his anxiety. He had said too many goodbyes in his short life. The reverend's parting was the last straw. He pondered over the reasons the reverend was called back to Europe. His immature brain attempted to make sense of it all. Some dim-witted chap in Germany hated the Jews. He planned to annihilate the entire race. How can anyone hate an entire community? Surely he must know that every community has good and bad people. Why kill the good ones? Jesus did not hate those who wronged him. Instead he asked God to forgive them. What right had this fool to hate and kill innocent people? He put the question before Reverend Beech. Beech explained that the world was full of people who abandoned God in preference of the devil. In return the devil promised them immense wealth and power. When such men attain power, it is time for all God's good men to get together and fight him. Why all God's good men did not prevent him from obtaining power in the first place, he was at a loss to understand. He concluded that the world must be full of fools.

In the midst of his musing, he recalled the old priest telling him that every person is born to fulfil a preordained destiny. One has a free will to fulfil or refute that destiny. If you defy it, it follows you into your next incarnation. Then the person is burdened with the karma of two incarnations. That is why some people remain unrewarded for their efforts. But God does not forsake any of his children. He decided to dedicate his entire life in search of his Goddess. He would find the statue and return it to his village. The intense reflection of past events made his adolescent brain weary and his eyelids heavy.

CHAPTER 2

Through the blur of tear filled eyes Gautam watched the reverend's car disappear into the distance. He returned to his room and grappled with a multitude of distressing emotions. He felt alone and abandoned. Baseless doubts and fears filled him with trepidation. For the first time in all these years, the walls of his room felt restrictive and stifling. The priests and staff did all they could to cheer him up, but his despondency persisted. He decided it was time to face his destiny. Gauging by all that he had heard, the world outside the mission was a daunting place. The priests advised him to wait a few more years. They said he was too young and innocent to face the trials and travails of the world outside. They warned him of bad people that took advantage of innocent. Procrastination was no longer an option. Before parting the reverend had given Gautam the wallet with ninety seven rupees and Travers' calling card. In addition he had given him the kingly sum of three hundred rupees as a parting gift. With three hundred and ninety seven rupees and the calling card he made his way to Howrah station. Brother D'Cruz was there to see him off.

Gautam alighted at Bombay's central station tired but elated. His plan was naively simple. All he needed to do was locate the address on the card, confront the monster and return with the Goddess. Dawn was still an hour away. Gautam whiled away the time observing the scene on the platform. It was not much different from the scene at Calcutta's Howrah station. It seemed to him that people on all stations were perpetually in a state of hurried frenzy. Gautam moved to one side of the platform to avoid being buffeted by the unruly crowds. The confused activity around him was exciting and awe inspiring. It suddenly dawned on him that the platform lay silent and deserted. The reality of the situation hit him like a speeding train. He was alone and vulnerable in an unknown city. The priest's stories of children being abducted, molested and forced into questionable trades made him uneasy. Anxiously he looked around to locate possible child abductors and molesters. He had no idea what molested meant, but it sounded frightening. To his relief the platform was devoid of individuals of any description. The absence of people was both reassuring and unnerving.

Gautam started to make his way towards the platform gate, alone and afraid. Finding the address created problems of its own. How was he to find the place without asking for directions? What if he approached the wrong kind of person and was kidnapped and molested? Trusting in his Goddess, he continued towards the gate. A powerful tug on the strap of his shoulder bag caused him stagger backwards and nearly fall. He turned to face a boy roughly his age. The stranger refused to release the shoulder strap. The boy was stronger than him. Gautam clutched the bag strap with all his might. All his belongings and his entire future was in that bag. Without it, he would be destitute. Worse, he would never find Mister Travers. It gave him added strength to fight back. He kicked wildly at the villain. The thief returned Gautam's kicks with a few punches. A blow on his chin caused him to almost pass out. But desperation gave him added strength. He was like a hungry fox fighting against a hyena for a juicy chunk of meat. The thief grabbed Gautam's fingers with his free hand to pry the strap out of Gautam's clasp. In desperation, Gautam blindly lashed out. His fist connected with the thief's wrist. The thief howled in pain and released his grip. He clasped his arm and doubled up in pain. Gautam noticed the boy was close to tears. Gautam gaped at his assailant flabbergasted. He noticed a deep gash that ran from the thief's wrist to halfway up his forearm. The sickening stench of a festering wound forced Gautam step back and cover his nose. Gautam had spent many hours in the infirmary of the mission hospital. He knew a wound like that required urgent attention. The two momentarily stared at one another in awkward silence.

The thief's scream brought a railway official rushing towards them. The official wore a sinister smile when he saw the thief. The young man had slipped through his fingers once too often. Gautam noticed the thief had turned deathly pale. He stood petrified with fear. Gautam guessed there was bad blood between the two. The official questioned Gautam about the incident. Gautam revealed that the boy offered to carry his bag for a fee. His hand accidently touched a festering wound on his arm. The official chuckled in response. 'This boy is known to have bested men twice his size in single combat. And you expect me to believe a slip of a boy like you made him scream in pain.'

'Believe what you want. I told you exactly what happened.'

'And you are?'

'My name is Gautam. I have just arrived from Calcutta, on that train sir.' He showed his ticket.

'It's been an hour since the train arrived. Why are you still here?'

'I was waiting for the time offices open. I have to find an address.'

The official rifled through Gautam's bag in the hope of finding something illegal. He watched anxiously as the official's fingers passed over Walsh's wallet. With a look of disappointment the officer ordered Gautam to vacate the platform. The official grabbed the thief by his injured arm. The villain screamed and almost passed out again. Gautam turned on the attendant like a vicious bull terrier.

'Are you a railway officer or a member of the Spanish Inquisition? Didn't I just tell you that my friend has a painful wound on his arm?'

The unexpected verbal assault took the official aback. 'Listen to me you little pipsqueak, I can make you disappear from the surface of the earth with a snap of my fingers' the official growled through clenched teeth

'And you listen to me you evil excuse of a man. I am here at the behest of one Mister Christopher Travers. He is expecting me at his office this morning. If I don't show up he will make enquiries. His enquiries will lead him to you. This coolie and I will inform him of your high handedness. There is every chance that you will cease to be an employee of the railways much longer. Now either you let my friend go or face the consequences.' To back his statement Gautam showed the official Travers's calling card. The officer had no clue of who or what the Spanish Inquisition could be. But he knew the name on the calling card. He turned and walked away muttering under his breath.

The young thief stood staring at the enigmatic stranger with a degree of admiration and bewilderment. He did not know what to make of the pint sized stranger. The half pint had displayed the tenacity and grit of a tiger. First he fought like one possessed for his little bag. Then he turned on the attendant with a barrage of abuses and accusations. Finally he produced a card that drained the blood from the officer's face. Around here such behaviour was regarded as suicidal. But the little fellow had saved him from the clutches of the most dreaded officer of the station. The runt had repeatedly referred to him as "my friend". No one had ever used that term in reference to him. He was grateful but suspicious. The mugger grew up in a world where people expected favour for favour. So far he had not hinted at anything in return. The runt could prove to be a worthy friend. Gautam tried to decipher the parade of expressions on the thief's face. He didn't learn much. But he felt an inexplicable connection with the mugger. They shook hands. The thief introduced himself as Ali. 'We must have a doctor examine that wound. It is festering. It could lead to amputation. I know, because I used to help the missionary doctors treat all kinds of wounds.'

'Are you mad? Doctors here charge two or three rupees, just to look at your face.'

'I'll pay.'

'Buy me breakfast instead. I haven't eaten anything since yesterday morning.'

'We will do both.'

Ali looked surprised. 'Who are you, the prince of Arabia?'

'Does one have to be the prince of Arabia to help others?'

'Ali could not contain his doubts any longer. 'If you are expecting anything in return, you will be sorely disappointed. I have nothing to give you.'

'I neither want nor expect anything from you. But what you said is not entirely true. You have friendship and love to give. These are two things that outweigh all the gold in the world.'

'What kind of love' Ali asked, fearing the worst.

'The kind of love one has for family and friends.' My father used to say that if a person needed help, it was your divine duty to do all you can for him. It seems our meeting was preordained.'

'Are you human or some heavenly spirit?'

Gautam laughed. 'We are all sprits from heaven draped in a myriad of earthly shapes.' Ali wasn't buying any of it. He remained suspicious of the benevolent stranger. But the temptation of a free meal was too much to resist. For Ali the meal was like a spread at a royal banquet. He wolfed down a full tandoori chicken. Then he devoured a plate of mutton and chapattis. He ended his meal with sweetened buttermilk. Gautam watched in awe as he struggled through his masala chicken.

'Now we find a doctor' Gautam said.

'The doctor can wait' Ali responded with a wave of the hand.

'You can wait, I can wait, the doctor can wait, but that wound cannot wait. I insist we have it attended to, right away. That is what I want in return for buying you breakfast.'

Ali screamed and cursed as the doctor treated his wound. The treatment took its toll on his strength and energy. He led Gautam to an old abandoned railway carriage. It had been his home for many years. A bedroll and a tin chest lay in one corner. The chest contained all of Ali's earthly possessions. The two boys whiled away the day relating their life stories. Ali had no memory of his mother. She died when he was only two years old. His father worked for a local gangster as an odd-job man. What he earned and how he earned it Ali could not say. His father was never a great provider but Ali was confident of two square meals a day. One day his father left home in the morning and never returned. Ali was just five years old. The local street vendors took pity on him. He was forced to run errands for them all day. Some of them were illegal. In exchange he received three meagre meals. They thrashed, insulted and verbally abused him for any mistakes. He endured it all for four terrifying years. He had no other option and nowhere to go. Then one day he got a lucky break. He was given ten rupees to buy opium. The opium vendor was located some distance away. Ali decamped with the money and arrived at Victoria station. Why he chose this particular station he had no idea. Employment evaded him in spite of all his efforts. The local hoteliers said he was too young to do anything. However they took pity on him. For a few years he survived on their hand outs. On days when the rush was overwhelming, they would permit him to do odd jobs for a paltry sum of money. He managed to keep body and soul together. Ali pointedly avoided revealing how he received the wound.

Gautam settled in his abandoned carriage home. Every morning Ali would leave to try and earn some money. Gautam would wander around, awed by the wonders of the city. He made sure to stay within the limits Ali had set for him. The multi-storied buildings, the hustle and bustle of city life, the variety of expensive items in shop windows, the tram cars, the horse-drawn carriages and the sight of automobiles enthralled him. He was truly enjoying himself. Every day introduced him to something new to see and learn. Thrilled by the sights and sounds of the city, his life's mission was transferred to the backburner.

Gautam sat with his legs dangling out of the carriage. He waited for Ali's return. That day Ali was late. The darkening shadows of twilight spread across the deserted yard. He started to worry. His imagination ran wild. He imagined the evil railway official held Ali in an unknown location. The thought sent him to the edge of panic. He pictured his friend lying beaten up in some deserted alley, crying out for help. He turned for succour from his Goddess. Gradually more calming thoughts replaced the terrifying scenarios. He realised the time had come to pursue his life's goal. He recalled the reverend saying that much delectation must be followed by much drudgery. He wondered if Ali would help or was he destined to leave another loved one behind. It surprised and amused him that he thought of Ali as a loved one. Their friendship was no more than a week old. But then, Ali was the only person in the world he could refer to as friend. Ali had become an integral part of his life. Gautam's musing ended with a powerful tug on his legs. He landed on his haunches with a thud. Gautam felt mind numbing pain shooting through his spine. The attacker kicked him in the ribs. The second man placed his foot on Gautam's neck.

'Hand over that bag or I'll squash you like a cockroach.'

Gautam clung to his bag like a new born monkey clings to its mother. His heart beat like a jungle drum and his limbs trembled like tuning forks. Relinquishing the bag was not an option he cared to consider. His determination was relentless. He searched for ways to try and save himself while the two assailants looked menacingly down at him.

The man applied more pressure on Gautam's throat. Gautam fought for breath. He believed these to be his last moments on earth. 'Give me that bag or----.' The man did not complete the sentence. The man cried in pain; arched his back and fell to his knees. Unknown to Gautam, Ali had delivered a powerful kick in the back of the bully's knee and followed with a kick in the kidneys. At the same time, Ali slammed his left elbow into the second man's face. Before either of the bullies could react, a shimmering cut-throat blade pressed against the throat of the kneeling bully. It all happened so fast, Gautam thought he was dreaming. All he could do was gape in disbelief.

'Tell your partner to go to the far corner of the yard now or I'll slit his throat.' Ali said threateningly. Ali waited for the second man to reach the far end of the yard. He then ordered the first man to stretch his arms and legs as wide as he could.' Ali kicked the man twice in his groin. The man grunted in pain, clutched his groin and doubled up. He followed with a kick in his throat. The man sank to the ground like a sack, coughing and groaning. Ali grabbed Gautam's arm and shouted at him to run as fast as he could. The man at the far corner chased after them. Every time Ali looked over his shoulder, the pursuer had gained ground. Ali pulled Gautam into an unlit cul-de-sac. They crouched behind a pile of refuse. 'You run like a sick snail' Ali whispered. The pursuer's shadowy form stopped just outside the alley. He entered the cul-de-sac like a stalking cat. Ali waited till their pursuer was within reach. He sprang into the air like a Jack-in-the-box with an ear piercing scream. He slammed his feet into the pursuer in the chest. The man staggered and struck his head on a stone wall. Ali grabbed the man's hair and repeatedly dashed his head against the wall. The man lay unconscious among the piles of garbage. Ali needed to choose between returning to the station and continuing on. Up ahead lay Chin Min's opium den. Returning to the station posed its own problems. If word had reached Chin Min, the station area could be swarming with his blood thirsty goons. Chin Min showed no mercy to anyone who defied him or his organisation. Ali opted to return to the station area. He knew every lane, gully and alleyway like the back of his hand. It offered far more opportunities to escape. They arrived at the yard. The area around his carriage home was devoid of goons. They pressed on till they were well away from the station.

'We managed to give Chin Min's men the slip. But we can never go anywhere near the station ever again' Ali said after they settled in a restaurant for some much needed refreshment.

'Who is this Chin Min?'

'He is the top don. All opium dens, gambling dens and whore houses in the area belong to him. Every other racketeer in the vicinity pays him a fee to do business.'

'What are opium dens and war houses?'

Ali could scarcely believe his ears. He wondered if Gautam pulling his leg.

'Places that have nothing to do with you.' Over tea and snacks they discussed their next move. Ali suggested they move to another city and set up a small shop, selling cigarettes, betel nuts and such. That was not an option for Gautam. The time to pay Travers a visit had arrived. He asked Ali to go with him. To his surprise Ali hesitantly agreed. He began to question Gautam.

'To whom does that card belong?'

'Mister Travers'

'And this Travers chap gave it to you?'

'No'

'Then how did you come to have it?'

'We found it in the murderer's wallet when the villagers searched the temple.'

'How did the murderer come to be in possession of the card?'

'I suppose Mister Travers gave it to him.'

'So there is a chance that this Travers chap could be the murderer?'

Gautam coughed out a laugh. 'This man's family donated the priceless statue to my village as a token of their gratitude. He has so much money he could make ten such statues if he wished. Besides, at the time of the temple incident, he was lying in the mission hospital, severely injured.'

Gautam related Travers' near fatal accident. It seems the wallet man survived the accident unharmed. He returned to the village to steal the statue. Ali hesitatingly agreed to accompany Gautam to Travers' office. They needed to find a place to spend the night. Ali knew of a number of cheap hotels but they all demanded rent.

'I have plenty of money' Gautam said out aloud.

Ali looked about him nervously. No one seemed to have heard his friend's faux pas. His friend's naivety was endearing but dangerous. 'Keep your voice down' he growled between clenched teeth.

The concierge of a disreputable hotel gave Ali a warm welcome. The two knew each other well. He looked at Gautam with a wry smile on his face. 'That's a change' he said, pointing to Gautam with his chin.

'This is my cousin from Calcutta. '

'Uh huh'

'This is his first visit to the city.'

'Uh huh, will that be two rooms or one?'

'One'

'Uh huh, Room seven. Hope your cousin enjoys his first visit' he said and winked.

When Gautam's back was turned Ali showed him the finger.

Ali turned on Gautam like a schoolmaster admonishing an errant student. 'You damned fool. Think before you say something in public. How much is lots of money?'

'Three hundred and seventeen rupees'

Ali could scarcely believe his ears. 'People around here disappear for as little as two rupees. These people are capable of killing a child just to get its sweets.'

Gautam offered to let Ali handle the finances. Ali flatly refused. 'If for any reason we get separated, you will be lost without it. For my part, I know how to survive in this world.'

Ali wrestled with the problem of a permanent residence. He placed the problem before Gautam. Gautam related his simplistic plan to confront the thief and recover the statue. After returning the statue to the villagers we come to Bombay and sought out the problem of finding a place to stay. There is an English saying, cross the bridge when you come to it.'

Ali gaped at his friend in wonderment. The boy truly had no concept of how the real world functioned. The possibility that the thief would flatly deny ownership of the statue did not even cross his mind. The possibility that two vagabonds could be denied entry into the office was not even considered. Gautam's reference to a bridge boggled him.

CHAPTER 3

Flora Fountain, the elite commercial district of Bombay stood in stark contrast to the station area. The buildings around the station were old and ill-maintained. The vicinity was littered and scruffy. The commercial district was spotlessly clean and boasted of handsome stone structures. Gautam was awestruck by everything around him. He felt he was transported to one of those cities in the reverend's magazines. The immaculately dressed men and large expensive cars left him awestruck. Even the security personnel were dressed in eye catching attires. The common man on the street, carrying briefcases and files walked at a dignified pace with a sense of purposeful urgency. The vendors too were well behaved.

Ali remained on tenterhooks. He believed that this part of town was not for the likes of him. The rule was simple. He was told that if you did not work here, you did not belong here. He had heard instances of wandering waifs facing the wrath of watchmen and policemen. Some of them were physically manhandled. His only experience with sahibs and memsahibs was at the station. They were by and large kind and generous. But this was not a railway station. This was a place where the overlords ruled supreme. His eyes shifted from side to side watching every watchman and passer by closely. Gautam's somnambulism irritated him. He behaved like one who had never seen human beings in his life. Ali walked close to the daydreamer. At the first hint of trouble, he was ready to grab Gautam and run. A passing Indian pedestrian returned Gautam's gape with a cold unfriendly stare. Every muscle in Ali's body remained primed for instant action.

Shortly before nine o'clock the huge teak doors of Travers' office building opened, signalling the start of the working day. A portly watchman guarded the Travers building entrance. He had about him the air of a Mogul general. Ali disliked his type. They were usually far more hostile than the sahibs. Soon men and women entered the edifice with an air of self-importance. Gautam prepared himself to confront his parent's murderer. The boys approached the entrance. Gautam portrayed self-confidence. Ali was nervous and wary. The portly guard stretched out his hand and arrogantly ordered them to stop. 'Where do you rascals think you are going?'

The man's supercilious attitude irked Gautam. 'It is not a matter of thinking. I know where I am going. I am going to meet Mister Christopher Travers.'

'Really, and I suppose that you are a business associate?' The guard sniggered mockingly.

'No, Mister Travers is a friend of my father.'

The exchange of words developed into a shouting match. Ali stood frozen to the spot. This was not the place for Gautam to lose his temper. It was one thing to confront a railway official, quite another to tussle with employees of the elite. Ali sensed the guard was about to use force. He readied himself to counter any possible assault. He assessed the man to be nothing more than a barrel of lard. The racket produced a tall, thin, stately lady. Her very presence would have sent Genghis Khan and Attila the Hun packing. The watchman's arrogance and hauteur dissipated. She enquired about the fuss in a voice that sent a chill up Ali's spine. 'This street urchin insists on meeting Mister Travers. I have been ordered not to permit any riff raff from entering the building.'

The glare with which the lady looked at Gautam made Ali weak in the knees. He gauged her to be the perfect antidote for Chin Min. She however had no such effect on Gautam. He drew Travers's card out of the wallet and shoved it under the lady's nose. Her jaw dropped when she saw the wallet. She seemed recognise it. The two boys were ushered into the office. Gautam thumbed his nose and poked out his tongue at the watchman as he strode past.

The woman's imperious and intimidating attitude had all but disappeared. The woman ordered tea and biscuits for the boys. She then disappeared into the bowels of the office. On her return she informed them that Mister Travers would be with them shortly. From time to time the woman glanced at the boys from over her horn-rimmed glasses. Ali pointedly avoided looking at her. He believed she must have last smiled when she was a baby. She reminded Gautam of Cruella Deville. 'If you start anything with this one you're on your own. I will be out of here faster than a speeding train' Ali whispered in Gautam's ear. The hubbub in the office died away. The staff busied themselves with the work at hand. A strikingly handsome man entered and threw a curious glace at the two scruffy boys. The man's gentle face and friendly demeanour had a calming effect on Ali's nerves. The moment Gautam saw Travers he jumped up and approached him with an extended hand. 'Mister Travers' he said, a bit too loudly, I don't know if you remember me. I am the murdered village priest's son.'

Travers shook the extended hand and patted the young visitor on the back.

'I remember you very well.'

Soon Harvey and Morrison joined Travers. The two late comers had an adverse effect on Ali. They seemed to have stepped out of a terrifying gangster movie. Gautam had a vague recollection of seeing Harvey before; the other man was a total stranger. Christopher asked Gautam how he came to possess the wallet. Gautam related the tragic temple incident in graphic detail. Travers and his associates sat in stunned silence. Even the terrifying secretary was visibly moved. Her eyes welled up with tears. Before leaving, Gautam mentioned that they had limited funds and nowhere to stay. Travers offered them accommodation in a room above his company's warehouse in the docks area. Christopher gifted each of them one hundred rupees and a daily stipend of ten rupees a day. The secretary returned Gautam's money but kept the wallet. Gautam was about to object but Ali nudged him to shut up. The receptionist delayed them a while longer. She rose from her chair like a wraith. Holding an empty glass bowl in her hand and demanded the attention of the entire staff. 'This young man has suffered more at this tender age than the rest of us have collectively. In this bowl I have placed five rupees. I will pass it around. I want to see it full of money when it is returned to me. I do not want to see any petty coins.' The staff responded to her command like obedient school children. The secretary noticed that Mister McGregor had slyly avoided making a donation. He considered it misguided generosity. She approached McGregor with bowl in hand. 'You must try to open your fist once in a while. It is good for the circulation.' The miser reluctantly placed a two rupees note in the bowl and proceeded to extract a rupee. The receptionist pulled the bowl away. 'That is enough exercise for one day.' The boys left the office with an additional amount of one hundred and eighty four rupees. On the way out Gautam and the watchman exchanged glares. An office employee escorted them to their new quarters. Later that day, they shopped for everything from hats to shoes.

Gautam was elated. Ali had concern stamped on his face. It perplexed Gautam. He questioned Ali about it. 'We are smack dab in the middle of Chin Min's domain of terror. Chin Min is a vindictive man. He never forgets or forgives.'

CHAPTER 4

Morrison suggested they visit Calcutta. Before leaving for Calcutta, Morrison and Harvey revisited Vajeshwari. Harvey harboured doubts about Pundit's claim that he had accidently stumbled on the priceless artefact. Now that Pundit was dead, the only person who could clarify the matter was Radhika. They met with Radhika at the Vajeshwari guest house. Radhika faced her interrogators with diffidence and apprehension. Morrison assumed the role of interrogator. In a soft gentle voice he requested her to repeat how her husband came to be in possession of the statue. Radhika related the incident exactly as her husband had told her. Harvey felt Morrison's velvet glove approach would not yield results. He decided to intervene. He slammed the coffee table with his fist and asked in a raised if she was certain he did not steal the statue. Harvey's unexpected reaction made Radhika and Morrison jump in their seats. Morrison very nearly upset his teacup. Radhika lost her composure. In a raised voice, she admitted her husband was guilty of many sins but assured them he was not a thief. Harvey continued with his Nazi style questioning. She burst into tears. She explained that if he was a thief, he would have sold it and lived the rest of his life in the lap of luxury. Why would he choose to endure the hardships of a remote village?

Harvey and Morrison arrived in Calcutta. Since the chief investigating officer was found dead in Vajeshwari, Detective Mather and the head constable Singh were the only ones who could throw any light on the matter. Mather explained the circumstances under which he got involved in the chase. He suggested that Constable Kamalbir Singh could give them more information. Morrison meticulously studied the case file. It provided no fresh clues.

Morrison insisted they pay the farm boy a visit. They learnt that the constable had settled on a remote farm. Harvey was familiar with the constable's conversational abilities. He knew what to expect. They found Kamalbir Singh on the veranda of his farmhouse, enjoying the warm summer breeze and a late morning cup of tea.

Singh sprang to his feet as the car entered the farm gate. His brain was a tangled knot of alarm and confusion. His heart beat like a jungle drum. A police Jeep in this rural setting could only mean serious trouble. He was certain Crowe was somehow involved. A wide range of spine chilling possibilities ran through his mind. The Jeep stopped right at the doorstep of his house. Two very officious looking men alighted from the car. Singh's heart missed a beat when he saw Harvey. The other man was a total stranger. In the absence of his wife he tried his hand at being a host. He nervously wondered if she knew how to play host to sahibs. Singh hadn't a clue what was expected of him. He sprang from his chair with an extended arm, tripped over a footstool, toppled the coffee table and almost flew into the arms of Morrison. He called out to his wife in sheer desperation. 'Summon the guests the servants have arrived' he shouted. He ordered Bunty the young help to bring the guests to water. He instructed the maid to bring snakes and teats for the guests. He started all over again but got so muddled that he ordered his wife to prepare Bunty for the maid. The wife arrived on the scene and put an end to her husband's comedy of errors with a glare. She graciously welcomed the unexpected visitors.

Morrison did not know what to make of the comical welcome. Harvey did not bat an eyelid. He looked forward to an entertaining afternoon. Morrison started the ball rolling. 'Do you recall Mister Travers's trip to a village in Bengal?'

'Yes I remember it very well.'

'I was told you were absent throughout the trip and the ceremony.'

'Yes sir, I was trailing chief inspector Crowe.'

The reply completely baffled Morrison. He attempted to simplify the question. 'The colonel reported that you were missing.'

'No, no, the colonel is mistaken. 'It was inspector Crowe's car that was missing. I was right there.'

Morrison glanced at Harvey, hoping for assistance. Harvey merely shrugged his shoulders and smiled mischievously.

Morrison guessed that he was wasting his time, however he persisted. 'Mister Singh, tell me everything from the time you went to the village to the very end.'

'You must bear in mind I was a mere constable' Singh said, in an attempt to absolve him of any blame. 'I was merely following the orders of my superior, inspector Crowe.' He then went on to relate the entire episode, starting from their initial trip to the moment the train carrying the criminal left Howrah station. Singh's narrative was exactly as it was in the case file. While recounting their discovery of the accident on the hill, Morrison noted Singh had provided an important detail.

'You say that you noticed expensive items strewn all over the place.'

'What did you infer from it?'

Singh took a while to guess what infer meant. 'I informed inspector Crowe.'

'Why did you not report this on your return to Calcutta?'

'That was up to inspector Crowe. I was not asked anything about it until the hearing.'

'What hearing?'

'Colonel Sahib knows about it.'

Harvey merely nodded affirmation.

'I suggest you speak to Crowe about this' Singh suggested.

'That would not be possible. Crowe is dead' Harvey said bluntly.

The news stunned Singh into a silent stupor.

The two investigators returned to Bombay, convinced that the elusive quarry was definitely on the Jhansi bound train when it left Howrah station. In Bombay they tried to trace the sequence of events that led to the statue ending up in Vajeshwari. They realised they were on a wild goose chase.

CHAPTER 5

Ali insisted they do not leave their residence after sunset unless it was absolutely necessary. The confinement started to tell on the boys. Gautam suggested they dine out. Ali was circumspect. He was circumspect. He reminded Gautam of Chin Min. As always Gautam got his way. Ali armed himself with a flick knife and a homemade cosh. He tucked the weapons under his trouser belt and threw on his recently purchased leather jacket. Gautam suggested they dine at one of the upper class restaurants.

The dockyard road was chock-a-block with heavy vehicles, cars, hand pulled carts and pedestrians. Every taxi that passed was engaged. The gaslights threw a pool of light directly under them. The space between the pools lay in relative darkness. A few lit windows in the commercial buildings gave the appearance of monolithic monsters watching them. Ali remained constantly on edge. He continuously looked over his shoulder. Gautam remained blissfully unaware of the dangers. As they approached the southern end of the road, the crowds had depleted. However they were still within Chin Min's sphere of terror. They encountered a handful of drunken sailors; a few families of street dwellers and a team of dock workers. Being a week day, the nocturnal revellers were noticeably absent.

Ali noticed four men standing idly at the corner, on the opposite side. One of them was the mugger at the abandoned carriage. He grabbed Gautam's arm and ordered him to keep looking straight ahead. The mugger spotted them and drew the attention of the others. They all turned and glared at them. Word of Ali's presence would surely reach Chin Min's ears. Men would soon be placed at strategic points.

Ali and Gautam stepped out of the restaurant after a hearty meal. Ali's nerves were on tenterhooks. He was well aware that word of his presence had reached Chin Min. As their taxi pulled up near the warehouse, two men emerged unnoticed from the shadows. Two men grabbed Ali while the third hit him hard over the head. Ali swayed and fell unconscious. A man holding a thick stick stood over him, seemingly proud of his accomplishment. The sight of Ali lying prostrate on the pavement brought out the tiger in Gautam. He turned on the truncheon wielder biting and kicking like one possessed. The assailants lifted him high in the air and slammed him against a stone wall. Gautam lay there limp and senseless.

When Gautam came to his senses, he found himself surrounded by a crowd of pavement dwellers. He searched for Ali among the crowd. Gautam was on the verge of hysteria. A compassionate pavement dweller advised him to forget the incident and return home. He warned that Gautam was dealing with very dangerous men. They added that his friend was probably already dead. Gautam offered fifty rupees to anyone who would take him to Chin Min.

The pavement dwellers responded with a laugh. They said they were not suicidal. Gautam begged them to at least guide him to the den. The beggars directed Gautam to a place called the Rice Bowl. Behind it lay Chin Min's den of sin. The beggars wished him good luck as Gautam walked away.

The Rice Bowl was a rickety tin shed that peeped through a row of equally rickety structures. Had he not been instructed he would have definitely walked past. The interior was just as shabby. A handful of young Chinamen were serving the few occupied tables. All the customers gaped in surprise to see a minor enter the place. Gautam chose a table close to the kitchen door. The unappetising aroma of cheaply prepared dishes wafted through it. He ordered a plate of sandwiches to avoid suspicion. He scanned the restaurant, searching for a place where they might be holding Ali prisoner. He recalled that the beggars referred to a place behind the restaurant. Gautam requested a waiter to show him the way to the toilet. A doorway behind the kitchen opened into a dark alley. It reeked of vomit and urine. Raucous sounds of merriment drifted to his ears from the far end of the alley. Gautam decided to investigate. He arrived at an open plot of land. A large group of men had formed a semicircle. Their attention was fixed on the centre. Catcalls, laughter and crude remarks filled the air. His heart beat wildly, believing that Ali's execution could be the main attraction.

But he was determined to save his friend. It gave him the courage to take a leap of faith. Gautam elbowed his way to the front of the crowd. The scene was reminiscent of a medieval public execution. The audience shouted insults, laughed at offensive jests and occasionally pelted Ali with lethal missiles. Ali stood stark naked in the centre with his hands and legs tied to a wooden stump. His face bled profusely. His naked body was covered with lash marks. His chin lay limp on his chest. A dwarf sized Chinaman entered the arena with the air of a medieval ruler. The cacophony died away. Complete silence fell on the proceedings. The medieval ruler spoke Hindi with a Chinese accent. His nasal twang pierced the night air like the screech of an eagle.

'So, this is the defiant pipsqueak' the Chinaman said, pulling Ali's limp head up by his hair. Where is your friend, partner or should I say lover?'

Peals of forced laughter rose into the night. Chin Min drew a long shimmering blade and menacingly held it close to Ali's throat. 'Should we start by skinning him, chopping his fingers and toes or just end it with swift decapitation?' A collective cry "skin him" rang out. A man from the semicircle joined the china man to assist in the torture. Chin Min looked directly at Ali's crotch. 'That's quite a trophy, let's cut it off and send it to his lover as a memento.' A cry of agreement rang out.

Gautam eyes remained fixed on the don. He noticed a butt of a gun jutting out of the Chinaman's hip pocket. Gautam had lost all sense of fear. He sprinted towards Chin Min, sprang forward like a predator and slammed his shoulder in the Chinaman's back. In one swift motion he grabbed the butt and took possession of the weapon. The crowd was stunned into silence. The onlookers gaped unbelievingly as Chin Min emitted a squeal of surprise and fell forward with his head at Ali's feet. Gautam pressed the barrel just under Chinaman's ear. The feel of cold steel knocked the wind out of Chin Min's sail.

'Tell your men to stay where they are. If I see any movement, you will find bits of your brain scattered all over the yard.' With the gun still pointing at Chin Min's bald head, Gautam ordered the volunteer to untie Ali. Ali slumped to the ground like a sack of potatoes. Ali's clothes lay in tatters on the ground. Gautam noticed a group of men inch towards the centre. He hit Chin Min's head with the butt of his gun. 'I told you to order them not to move' he shouted. Chin Min ordered his gang of goons to stay where they were. They stepped aside, creating a wide passageway to the restaurant. Gautam ordered the volunteer to assist Ali to the restaurant. Crockery and cutlery slipped from some of the waiter's hands when they saw the boss enter as a prisoner of a child. The customers gaped unbelievingly. He warned the waiters not to attempt any heroics. Gautam selected a waiter roughly Ali's height and build and ordered him to strip. The waiter hesitated. Chin Min ordered him to do as he was told with an ear splitting scream. There was unmistakable fear in his voice. With trembling hands the waiter dressed Ali. Chin Min ordered his men to back away from the entrance. The men followed them with their eyes as the three made their way to the main road. None dared move, fearful of their boss's wrath.

They hailed a passing taxi. The cabbie recognised the don and refused the fare. Gautam showed him the gun. Chin Min was made to sit in front next to the driver. Gautam sat directly behind his hostage with the barrel pressed into back of Chin Min's head. The Chinaman sat frozen with fear. Gautam ordered the cabby to stop in a particularly dark area of the road. He made Chin Min step out of the cab, removed the bullets and threw the gun at his head. They spent the night in the out-patient ward of a Hospital.

CHAPTER 6

Harvey and Morrison visited the address in Koran found in Vajeshwari. They received a cold welcome. A worker rudely told them to wait in the congregation hall and disappeared. The imam made an appearance after a considerable period of time. His manner was brusque. Harvey presented the imam with the bag and the Koran. The imam denied he had ever seen the bag but accepted ownership of the Koran. He said it could belong to any of the clerics. The imam stood up, indicating an end of the meeting. Harvey said a gun was found in the bag. He watched closely for the imam's reaction. The man was visibly ill at ease. The imam vociferously denied any knowledge of a gun and asked to see it. Morrison said the forensic department had taken it for examination. The mention of police further unnerved the imam. The imam walked away, ordering them to leave the bag and the Koran. Harvey refused to comply. He said that the items were found at a crime scene in Vajeshwari. The imam thanked them for their trouble and requested them to leave. The two sleuths left the mosque none the wiser.

CHAPTER 7

Christopher spent most of his time alone in his home. He had not heeded the old priest when he said that the Goddess had a preordained agenda for the statue. Now he could see the truth in his words. Christopher ordered Harvey and Morrison to end their search.

It grieved Harvey and Morrison to see their boss suffer. Travers answered a phone call and handed it to Morrison after a brief hello. All Morrison said was 'I see' and 'thank you.' He caller informed Morrison that the gun was indeed the one used in the Vajeshwari murder. The owner of the weapon is one Rafiq Ali Khan.

The news stunned Christopher. The alleged owner was a gentleman of high standing. He knew the man well. It would be embarrassing to confront him without proof of his involvement. They finally convinced Christopher to meet the man and see what he had to say. Christopher secured an invitation from Rafiq Ali Khan. Khan's sprawling bungalow sat nestled in the centre of an immaculately manicured garden. Marble statues of Greek Gods and Roman warriors lined a cobbled driveway. A tall powerfully built domestic aide led them into an opulent living room, adorned with Persian carpets, Victorian furniture and a vast collection of Chinese and Italian porcelain antiques. Khan warmly welcomed Christopher and his two companions. Uniformed waiters constantly went around offering caviar on toast and smoked salmon sandwiches. Brazilian coffee and Earl Grey tea, poured out of highly polished silver pots. The waiters were on call at all times. Havana cigars lay in silver humidors, waiting to be taken. After introductions and a bit of small talk, Christopher diplomatically steered the conversation to the matter at hand. He told Khan that a weapon belonging to him was found at a crime. Morrison placed the weapon on the coffee table. Khan examined it and denied it belonged to him. He said he did not own thirty two calibre weapons. Morrison tactfully questioned their host further. The interrogation put Khan in a spot of bother. Khan suddenly recalled gifting the gun to the imam of his mosque. It was what Morrison was hoping to hear. Morrison sensed a degree of unease in his host's demeanour. He risked pressing Khan for a bit more information. Harvey noted that the host was starting to get uncomfortable. Morrison would have preferred to pursue the matter, believing that he could trick Khan into divulging a few more important bits of information. But Khan excused himself remembering a previous engagement. It brought the tea party to an end. Later Rafiq Ali Khan barged into the mosque to confront the imam. He chastised the imam for giving the cleric his gun. He called the cleric an irresponsible fool. The imam placed the blame squarely on the shoulders of the evil imam of Lahore. He reminded Khan how dangerous it was to disobey his orders. He philosophised that the deed had been done and the die had been cast.

The imam's short discourse confounded Khan. He asked how the imam proposed to undo a murder and the theft of a national treasure. He warned he would not lift a finger to assist. Khan sent an express telegram to Rahim, his most trusted employee. He ordered Rahim to inform the evil imam to confiscate the statue and the gun and revoke the cleric's membership of Womb.

****

In Christopher's office they discussed Rafiq Ali Khan. Christopher refused to believe that his friend could in any way be involved in a crime. He insisted that the meeting revealed no implicating evidence. Morrison pointed out that Khan had contradicted himself throughout the discussions. Finally the man had abruptly ended the meeting. Harvey agreed with Morrison. Travers asked what they proposed to do next. Morrison was convinced that the cleric was still in possession of the statue. He suggested they follow him to Lahore. Travers' mood changed from despondent to dramatic. He ordered Harvey and Morrison to get off their arses and catch the first train to Lahore. He warned them not to return without the statue. He ordered them to shoot the cleric if necessary.

CHAPTER 9

Ali and Gautam decided to spend the day outdoors. They visited Mahalaxmi temple, the zoo, the gateway of India, Juhu beach and Apollo Bunder. Bombay being the commercial and financial hub of India, it had little else to offer by way of interest to adolescent tourists. At the gateway, Gautam stood in awe and gaped at the grandeur and majesty of the Taj Mahal hotel. The lengthening evening shadows prompted Ali to head home. For once Gautam did not argue.

Back in their room, Gautam spent his time in pursuit of teachings of the Gita. His adolescent mind could only grasp bits and pieces of the profound scripture. Ali concentrated on his physical fitness. Mentally exhausted, Gautam set aside the text and admired Ali's physique.

The following day, they visited Travers' office to collect their monthly stipend. The receptionist was responsible for all of Gautam's needs. She welcomed them with a cheerful smile. While waiting for the receptionist to complete the paperwork, Gautam's ears picked up Christopher's raised voice. The words Lahore, statue and cleric piqued his interest. They left the building financially fortified. Ali suggested they lunch at a restaurant that served the most delectable Muslim food. He found Gautam in a world of his own. Ali was forced to repeat his suggestion. Gautam agreed with an absent minded nod.

The restaurant was situated in the infamous red light area. The vicinity abounded with undesirable characters. Ali warned Gautam not to daydream or stare at anyone or anything. He took possession of the money. He divided the notes and shoved them in different pockets. As they exited the restaurant, Ali felt a strong tug on his arm. He turned like a spinning top, his right arm ready to throw a punch. He recognised an old friend just in time. Ali's reaction brought to mind the Chin Min episode. Gautam sprang on the stranger like one possessed. He clawed and kicked for all he was worth. It took a concerted effort by Ali to pry Gautam away. A large crowd gathered round them. Ali was apprehensive. In this part of town, a crowd meant trouble. Ali and his friend played down the incident. The crowd dispersed disappointed. Ali was proud that his lion hearted friend had come to his defence once again.

After lunch, Gautam insisted they return to Travers's office. They entered the boss's plush cabin. Travers welcomed them with a broad smile. Gautam sat silent, fidgeting with his shirt sleeve and staring at the Persian carpet. He mentally reprimanded himself for his impulsiveness. After a bit of coaxing from Travers, Gautam found the nerve to speak. He stuttered and stammered as he requested a loan of one thousand rupees. Gautam explained that it would soon be the old priest's death anniversary. He wished to make a donation and take gifts for the villagers. Without a moment's hesitation, Travers ordered the receptionist to give him the money.

Ali could not contain his curiosity. He questioned Gautam about the humungous loan and the trip to his village. Gautam replied that they were not going to his village, they were going to Lahore. Ali gaped, believing his friend had lost his mind. Gautam explained that he always heeded his instincts. His instincts had urged him to leave the sanctuary of the mission hospital and pursue his life's goal. He did not find the statue, but he did find the best friend anyone could hope for. Now they were telling him to go to Lahore. He averred that he would not reverse his decision. Finally he asked if Ali would accompany him. Ali hesitatingly agreed.

CHAPTER 10

Gautam and Ali stepped off the train at Lahore station. They spotted Morrison and Harvey in the company of two strangers. The boys saw them drive away in a large black car. They finally found a suitable hotel in the marketplace. It was within walking distance from the station. Ali felt it was a necessary precaution in the event they needed to flee. After a refreshing bath and dinner they both fell into a deep dreamless slumber. Over breakfast they discussed their first course of action. As coming to Lahore was Gautam's idea, Ali left the planning to his friend. He enjoyed seeing Gautam struggle for ideas. For over an hour Gautam made a series of unviable suggestions. Finally Ali assumed control.

The concierge guided them to a mosque within walking distance from their hotel. After dodging their way through the crowds and unruly traffic they arrived at the mosque. Ali peered through the partially open front door. The entrance hall was large, dimly lit and unoccupied. He called out in a raised voice. A boy roughly their age appeared out of nowhere. He was frail, shy and seemingly insecure. Ali glared at the boy and spoke in a voice that exuded confidence and authority. Ali told the boy that they were from Bombay and needed assistance. The boy left to fetch an elder. Ali was wary of elders. They tended to ask too many questions. After a long while, they heard the distinct shuffle of feet. In the dim interior, Gautam could only discern the outline of someone or something drifting towards them. Its pace was exasperatingly slow. The apparition seemed to have neither a head nor limbs. The sight told made Gautam edgy. His jaw dropped, his temples throbbed, and beads of sweat formed on his brow and upper lip. He was ready to flee. He sidled up to Ali for reassurance. Ali sat calmly without batting an eyelid. At last the apparition appeared in its entirety. It was the imam of the mosque. He welcomed them with a cheery toothless smile and asked how he could help. Ali explained he had lost his uncle's address. The imam questioned Ali about his uncle. Ali said his uncle was a carpenter named Mohamed Khan. The imam laughed and said there must be hundreds of carpenters with the same name. He peppered Ali with a series of unrelated and inconsequential questions. Ali suspected the old man was playing for time. He thanked the imam and made for the entrance. He pushed Gautam ahead of him. They left the mosque none the wiser.

On Gautam's insistence, they decided to visit another mosque. This time they needed to hire a hand pulled rickshaw. At the end of a journey that entailed death defying encounters with cars, busses and trucks, they pulled up outside the entrance of a much larger mosque. Ali knocked on a huge ornately carved wooden door. It was answered by what at first glance appeared to be an alien. The hulk glared down at them through saucer sized eyes. He did not utter a word. Ali said he wished to speak to the imam. The creature responded with a blank stare. Then he raised the palm of his hand and disappeared into an inner chamber of the mosque. Gautam lost his nerve. He was anxious to leave. For what seemed an eternity, they saw no sign of the giant or anyone else. Suddenly a high pitched voice reverberated in the confines of the waiting room. The two boys jumped skyward. A creature with a shrivelled prune like face; beady eyes and a beak of an eagle appeared out of nowhere. Ali studied the face closely. He could discern an extremely sharp and cunning mind. The creature's eyes shifted from Ali to Gautam constantly. He asked how he could help. Once again Ali repeated the tale of his uncle's lost address. The prune fixed a nerve wrecking glare on Ali. 'This is not a public information bureau' he croaked. The statement rattled Gautam. He gave the imam a brief lecture on the duties of priests of all religions. The silence that followed was long and nerve wrecking. The old man's stare grew colder and more intense. He was clearly weighing his options. He requested the boys to wait while he made enquiries. His tone of voice was friendly and courteous. The sudden change of attitude set off alarm bells in Ali's head. He noticed the imam give the monster an imperceptible nod. Ali feared some sinister game was afoot. He indicated to the giant that he wanted water. The giant seemed confused. On the one hand he had to follow the imam's orders. On the other, he could not refuse a guest a glass of water. It was morally and ethically wrong. Seeing that the giant was hesitant to grant his request, Ali searched for something to distract the monster. His eyes fell on a corner table with a metal flower vase on it. The table stood a few feet away from the entrance. He nonchalantly inched towards the table with Gautam close behind. Ali spun around like a pirouetting ballerina and flung the vase at the giant. The monster's agility left a lot to be desired. The vase slammed into his face. Ali grabbed Gautam and sprinted towards the entrance door. The two boys were out of the mosque well before the monster recovered. The monster charged after them like an enraged rodeo bull. He barged through a crowd of irate pedestrians. The giant stumbled and crashed to earth like a felled tree. His face was buried in a mound of cow dung. The street urchins could not resist ridiculing the fallen giant. The monster sheepishly made his way back to the mosque, seething with rage. Back in the hotel, Ali opined that it was best they leave Lahore. Gautam begged for one more chance. Ali agreed, on the condition that they return to Bombay in the event they ran into trouble again. They shook hands over the deal.

CHAPTER 11

The Travers reputation and influence stretched the full length of the sub-continent. Harvey and Morrison received commissionaire of police's full cooperation. They had a sizable contingent of the force at their beck and call. However, more than fifty per cent of officers and constables were Muslims. Harvey doubted they could induce them to arrest a Muslim cleric. The day for Indian Independence and partition loomed ever closer. Neither the Hindus nor the Muslims regarded the British as overlords. Morrison gave a long stirring speech, before informing them of plan. The Muslims discussed the matter and flatly refused to cooperate. Morrison was not one to let a setback dampen his resolve. Though they were left with less than fifty per cent of their allotted force, he decided to soldier on. It seemed fate was doing all it could to favour the damn cleric. First they needed to ascertain in which mosque the cleric resided. Then they needed to find an excuse to meet and interrogate him. Harvey and Morrison were not men to let grass grow under their feet. They discussed the matter with Barclay the police commissionaire.

CHAPTER 12

Gautam and Ali stood at the window admiring a colourful parade. Deafening sounds of exploding firecrackers filled the air. A band of gaudily attired musicians played music that only added to the cacophony. The crowd seemed to enjoy it. Teenage boys and girls danced to the inharmonious rhythm. The grownups wholeheartedly urged them on. The exuberance of the crowd was infectious. Ali and Gautam decided to take a closer look. The concierge informed them that the celebrations were for the birth of separate Muslim state. India was going to be divided into two countries. The news effected Gautam adversely. He grieved over the partition of his country. He considered the Muslims as ingrates. Ali feared that as a Muslim he may be forced to remain here.

The rejoicing had infested the lobby. It resounded with catcalls, raucous laughter, crude language and lewd jokes. They entered the dining room for breakfast. It was packed to capacity. A waiter ushered them to a table already occupied by two other teenagers. They shook hands, exchanged pleasantries and fell into mundane conversation. One of the strangers entertained them with a succession of jokes. Ali noticed that the joker's attention was focused on Gautam. Gautam's guffaws only served to encourage the clown. Ali suspected the boy of evil intentions. The presence of women and children forced Ali to restrain his anger. Besides, the strangers may have friends around. In a free for all, Gautam would be as useless as a mouse in a cat fight. Suddenly Gautam excused himself to answer the call of nature. The obvious bulge in his trousers drew stares, winks and whistles. Ali too could not restrain a smile. The pervert got up and followed Gautam into the toilet. When Ali entered the men's room, he found the debauchee forcing himself on Gautam. 'Take your filthy hands off him.' The joker drew a knife from his pocket and advanced, backing Ali into a corner. Ali had no option but to attack. He leapt at the pervert like a jaguar. The joker backed away with equal agility. Ali slipped and fell. The villain knelt on Ali and raised his hand to plunge the knife into Ali's chest. The joker inexplicably swayed like a palm tree and crashed to the floor. Gautam stood over him with a heavy brass bucket in his hand. When Gautam stepped into the dining room, he was still the centre of attention.

CHAPTER 13

Morrison and Barclay were left with just thirty per cent of the police force. They needed to keep a twenty four seven watch on all the mosques in the city. It seemed an impossible task. They discussed a number of alternate plans. Each one posed its own problems. Finally they decided to send a couple of men to each mosque disguised as press photographers. For weeks Barclay, Morrison and Harvey scrutinised every photograph. Most of the were familiar to Barclay. However, one unknown face drew his attention. His enquiries revealed that the man had only recently arrived in Lahore. The vendors, beggars and urchins had dubbed him the crazy cleric. Constables were told to tail the man twenty four seven. A week later the constables reported that their quarry had gone missing. It was a severe blow.

Barclay received a complaint by a Hindu priest registered at a suburban police station. It was reported that an unknown cleric regularly abused Hindu priests and intimidated the residents. The cleric boasted that soon Islam would be the only religion in the world. He professed the end of the Hindu religion. They would be given the choice to convert or die. The suburban police were hesitant to use force. They asked for advice. Under normal circumstances, the matter would have been labelled as trivial and shelved. But the description, unknown cleric, demand urgent enquiry. Harvey and Morrison visited the village. They could feel the tension. They met the Hindu priest who had lodged the complaint. He was seething with indignation. He was prepared to publicly identify the cleric regardless of the consequences.

Barclay knew that they needed prior permission to enter the mosque. He shelved the idea of a police raid. Arresting the cleric without proof of a crime was out of the question. It would lead to litigation. The governor would come down on him like a ton of bricks. Harvey suggested they abduct the cleric. Harvey approved the idea but Barclay was dead set against it. 'This is not a Hollywood gangster movie' Barclay reprimanded. Morrison and Harvey plotted to kidnap the cleric without Barclay's knowledge. However they needed to get acquainted with the man's daily routine. For that they needed policemen. To engage policemen they needed Barclay's permission. They were back to square one.

Barclay received a phone call from a police officer reporting that the face they were after was among a large group of people waiting at the entrance of the main mosque. Harvey and Morrison raced to the mosque in Barclay's Ford Prefect. From the behaviour of the group it was apparent that someone important was due to arrive. Harvey and Morrison watched the proceedings from inside their car. Bored, Harvey turned his attention to the activity on their side of the road. He noticed two boys ambling towards them. All their attention was riveted on the activity outside the mosque. However, they appeared apprehensive. They constantly took cover behind letterboxes and trees. The face of the smaller boy seemed vaguely familiar but he could not place him. He dug deep into his memory cells to recall where he had seen it before. Harvey's preoccupation with the boys was intruded upon by a nudge from Morrison. He turned in time to see a black Daimler glide noiselessly past them and halt at the entrance of the mosque. Mohamed Ali Jinnah and Rafiq Ali Khan alighted from the car. Khan's presence forced them to put their plan on hold. Khan would have no trouble recognising them. An Austin van pulled up behind the Daimler. Two men emerged from the Austin. Harvey could tell the first man had a military background. The second was a monolithic monster. The man with a military background scanned every square inch of the neighbourhood. The monolith merely stood and gaped about him stupidly. His obvious physical power was not lost on either of them. Something clearly agitated the monster. He dashed across the road like a starving carnivore spotting potential prey. Members of the crowd ran in all directions to avoid the beast. Harvey noticed the look of terror on the faces of the two boys. The monster had both the boys in his grasp. Harvey was not willing to watch two adolescent boys beaten to a pulp by a sub-human entity. He leapt out of the car and ran to assist the youngsters. Morrison followed his colleague. He feared that the monster would tear his partner to ribbons.

CHAPTER 14

Gautam's sulking melted Ali's heart. He agreed to visit one more mosque. The bellboy suggested they visit Lahore's main mosque. They would need to hire a horse drawn buggy to get there. The four legged somnambulist plodded along at a painfully slow pace. Close to the main mosque, they ran into a traffic jam. The driver suggested they walk down a lane that led to the mosque. They reached the end of the lane and found themselves on an equally chaotic road. The mosque stood on the opposite side of the road. A group of people had gathered outside the entrance. The group eagerly stepped off the kerb every time they spotted an expensive car. An irate driver swerved and went straight for the crowd, causing them to scatter in every direction. The street urchins, vagabonds and vendors jeered the welcoming party. Gautam watched the event thoroughly amused. Ali studied the scene with intense concentration. Two vendors close to them passed derogatory remarks about a member of the group. Gautam's ears picked up the word cleric. After a brief exchange of friendly chatter, Ali brought the topic round to the cleric in question. He asked them to identify the man. The vendors brazenly pointed to a frail anaemic looking man. Ali studied the man closely. He appeared to be in the throes of an epileptic fit. His fingers constantly fidgeted; his face muscles twitched, alternating between a smile and a frown. He found it difficult to stand in one place for more than a few minutes.

Gautam was fascinated by the row of expensive cars parked along the kerb. They were all shiny and new. Among the impressive fleet of cars, Gautam noticed an old Ford Prefect. It reminded him of reverend Beech's car. He noticed a card on its windshield that read "Press" in bold letters. He briefly wondered how anyone could achieve such a feat. Gautam soon lost interest in the car and the word.

Gautam and Ali noticed a giant of a man charging in their direction. They instantly recognised him. Their attempt to flee was in vain. The monster was already on to them. He lifted Gautam off the ground and threw him several feet across the pavement. Incensed, Ali threw caution to the wind and sprang at the monster. He took a wild swing at the monster's groin but missed his mark. The monster grabbed Ali by the neck and shook him like a ragdoll. Ali was struggling to breathe. Much to his surprise and relief, he saw Harvey in the corner of his eye.

Harvey slammed into the monster's back and punched him several times in his kidneys. The giant turned with the agility of a tired tortoise, livid and bewildered. Harvey realised he could not afford to lose the advantage. He lifted his knee in the monster's groin and followed with a punch in the monster's throat. The monster emitted a deep groan of pain; covered its face with its hands and staggered backward but remained standing. Harvey stepped back to avoid an arm as thick as a lamp post aimed at him. He felt the rush of wind as the sledgehammer like fist missed his face by mere inches. He ducked and landed a two handed punch in the monster's face. The blow should have rendered him senseless. He merely wiped the blood from his torn lip and lunged forward growling like an enraged grizzly. He grabbed Harvey with both arms, lifted him and threw him several feet through the air. The monster charged at Harvey again. He grabbed Harvey's lapels and slammed him repeatedly against the wall. Harvey cupped the monster's face with both hands and dug his thumbs into its eyes with all his might. He followed with a head butt on the bridge of the monster's nose. The monster's knees buckled. He bent over, cupping its throbbing private parts and groaning. The monster reeled and hit the ground like a felled tree. The entire welcoming committee stared in disbelief. Harvey scanned the length and breadth of the by lane for the boys. They seemed to have vanished into thin air. He noticed the military man race across the road. He was too old to take on a younger military trained man. He hurried to the car as fast as he could. Morrison shouted the driver to speed away. The military man ran to the car and managed to grab the door handle. But the Ford Prefect lurched forward and gathered speed. Morrison saw the military man wring his hand in pain. They related the entire episode to Barclay.

The sight of the two boys plagued Harvey. He pondered over the likelihood of Gautam and Ali's presence in Lahore. The uncanny resemblance went beyond the realm of coincidence. Doubt and suspicion entered his mind. He recalled that Gautam and Ali had dropped into Travers office out of the blue. They could have accidently stumbled upon Walsh's wallet where Pundit stumbled upon the statue. Travers's calling card guided them to the office. They might have decided to visit the office in the hope of a sizable hand out. So they invented Gautam's cock and bull story. Harvey recalled that Gautam had asked for a thousand rupees. Soon after, they disappeared. Now they were in a Muslim dominated city clad in Muslim attire. The pieces seemed to fit. The boys were members of a gang that had stolen the statue. Harvey voiced his concerns to Morrison.

Morrison looked at his partner exasperated. He advised that Harvey should think things through before he spoke. He opined that the hypothesis had several contradictions. Firstly, the wallet proves that Walsh was involved in the theft of the statue and possibly the murder the priest and his wife. Secondly, if the boy resided in Bombay, how could he have known of the murders? Thirdly, Travers recognised the boy. Thirdly, if the boys were part of a clan that had stolen the statue, why would they bother to visit the office for a hand out? Lastly, why would the monster attack members of his own clan? Harvey conceded that Morrison's argument made sense.

CHAPTER 15

The cleric's jaw dropped when he saw his champion bodyguard defeated by an Englishman twice his age. He summoned his small group of followers into his chamber. It included the giant. He agitatedly paced the floor in anger, throwing objects every which way. His followers ducked and swayed to avoid the flying missiles. Finally he stopped his pacing. 'I have been chosen by Allah and the prophet to convert the world to Islam. You are fated to be the pioneering champions of this noble cause. But sadly we are riddled with incompetence. I submit before you this subhuman gorilla. He can effortlessly lift three hundred pounds with one hand. Tear car licence plates. He has defeated two, two hundred and fifty pound wrestlers, singlehanded. But when it came to proving his worth, he was incapable of handling an Englishman half his size and twice his age. This is unacceptable. The cleric ordered his commander-in-chief to find and bring the Englishman and the two teenage boys dead or alive to the mosque. Failure was punishable by death he warned.

'I can tell you about the two Englishmen' a refined voice said. Everyone turned to face Rafiq Ali Khan. He had appeared in the midst of the gathering unnoticed. Khan informed them that the one who laid the giant cold is a highly decorated retired colonel of the S.A.S. The other is a top rate Scotland Yard detective. They are both currently employed by Christopher Travers of Travers Corporation. Their job is to trace and retrieve a gold statue of a Hindu Goddess believed to be worth millions. It was recently stolen from a remote village in the suburbs of Bombay.' The cleric could scarcely believe his ears.

He wondered why Khan had willingly made such sensitive information public. But he did not have the courage to question the head of Womb.

The cleric hurried away to consult with the evil imam. The man disliked being kept in the dark about anything. The cleric informed the imam that he had ordered the two Englishmen and the boys to be brought in for questioning. The imam chided him for assuming authority. The cleric reminded the imam that in his opinion he was a hunted man. The imam dismissed the cleric's doubts and fears as unfounded. Before dismissing the unwanted intruder, the evil imam reminded the cleric that his absurd belief he was Allah's chosen one was merely an illusion.

The cleric returned to his room. His men were waiting for him. He harboured ill feelings about the evil imam and Khan. He waited for the day he would see them beg for mercy. But that was all in the future. First he needed to find a way to protect himself from meddling Englishmen and the enigmatic boys. He asked the commander if he had formulated a plan. The commander tried to wash his hands off the entire affair. He recommended Rahim as a more suitable choice. The cleric reaction was that of a man who had been electrocuted. He vibrated from stem to stern. He proclaimed Rahim to be Khan's puppet. He feared Rahim would place the men and boys squarely in Khan's lap. The cleric insisted the commander execute the capture. The commander asked for a larger task force. The cleric exploded like a stick of dynamite. When I give an order I expect it to be carried out without question' the cleric screamed. It dawned on the cleric that the monster was the only one of his men who could recognise the two boys. He had no choice but to reemploy the monster.

CHAPTER 16

Gautam and Ali sprinted into a lane to escape the giant. They watched Harvey fight the monster from behind the trunk of a large tree. Both the boys were thrilled to see Harvey gain the upper hand. Gautam clapped when a gang of mosque's workers carried the monster away. But then a muscle bound man arrived on the scene. They had seen the man arrive at the mosque in the company of the giant. Thankfully the muscleman's attention was focused on the Englishman. They hid behind a large banyan tree.

Ali found Gautam staring open mouthed at something behind him. He turned and saw an old man with radiant skin and a long flowing beard standing over them. His skin appeared to glow. He held a string of prayer beads in his hand. Absolute fear gripped Ali. He believed the bearded stranger to be a resident of the mosque. Ali stood to defend himself. The stranger held his hand over Ali head and gave him a reassuring smile. Miraculously Ali's fear subsided. Both boys noticed that the din of the street had died away. The rushing crowds and buildings seemed to have mysteriously vanished. The tree, the bearded stranger and they were the only ones in the lane. Gautam believed they had stepped through a time warp. The enigmatic stranger started to speak. 'Let your heart not your head to guide you' the old man said to Ali. He lectured Ali on the evils of violence. He related Ali's past in detail. The phantom turned his attention to Gautam. He praised Gautam's loyalty to the Goddess, but chastised him for his deception and lies. Gautam guessed the phantom was referring to the loan of the thousand rupees. It was the only lie he had ever told. He then related Gautam's entire life. The phantom smiled when he saw the astonished look on the faces of both boys. He foretold that the boys will soon have to part ways. Both of them will face trouble and strife. In God's good time they will find each other again. But the reunion will be short lived. However, their souls will be bound together throughout eternity. That is the will of the Supreme Being. Gautam gripped Ali's hand like a frightened child. He looked at the strange being with tear filled eyes. 'Wipe those tears. Be strong and always trust in God. We all have to succumb to his will. It is best we do it with faith and fortitude.'

The apparition vanished as mysteriously as it had appeared. The sights, sounds and smells of the lane awoke their mortal senses. They looked dumbly at each other and everything around them, as though they were seeing the world for the first time. No one seemed to be aware of the mystical event that had occurred. The boys looked up and down the street for an old man with a string of beads. They saw neither hide nor hair of him. It seemed to them that the entire experience was a figment of their collective imaginations. Neither the pragmatic Ali nor the theosophical Gautam could offer a logical explanation.

Ali noticed the ice cream vendor quizzically stare at them. Ali ordered two ice cream sticks to lure the vendor into a friendly conversation. He started with small talk. Then he introduced the matter of their experience. The vendor avoided answering Ali's questions. Gautam asked if the vendor had noticed anything strange about the street. The vendor hesitatingly admitted that he believed the two of them had lost their minds. They were talking to a tree. He admitted that if this happened after sunset, he would have fled faster than a bullet leaving a gun. He said the tree was rumoured to be haunted. People have experienced all manner of bizarre occurrences. 'Where did the old man go?' Ali asked.
'What old man?'
A chill ran down Gautam's spine.

CHAPTER 17

Harvey continued to mull over the presence of Gautam and Ali in Lahore. He continued to believe the boys were somehow involved with those who stole the statue. He concluded that the only way to solve the mystery was to capture the boys and interrogate them. Finding them posed a number of problems. He was at a loss to decide where to start his search. Moreover, he would need the chief's cooperation. Barclay was not one to bend the law. He took a chance and told the commissionaire of the two boys. Barclay rejected the idea outright. He was not prepared to kidnap two minors, as there was no proof of any criminal activity. Harvey convinced Morrison to join him in the quest. He informed Morrison that Gautam borrowed a thousand rupees from Travers. The boy had said he wished to visit his village. The amount surprised Morrison. Morrison suggested the station area would be the best place to start. He guessed that they must have rented a room in a cheap hotel. He reasoned that streetwise lads like them would prefer to stay close to the station.

CHAPTER 18

Rafiq Ali Khan was certain that Harvey and Morrison were in Lahore to retrieve the statue. They could easily trap the imbecile cleric if they cross questioned him. He could reveal the existence of Womb. He ordered his henchmen in the police force to inform him of Morrison and Harvey's residential address. It was imperative he get hold of the hounds before it was too late. Khan regarded Gautam and Ali as inconsequential. They could not possibly pose a threat. However, he decided it would do no harm to know why they decided to visit Lahore. He saddled Rahim with the additional task of finding the boys.

Khan's moles learnt that Harvey and Morrison resided at the government guest house. They conducted their business from the police headquarters. Khan used his considerable influence to have Barclay transferred to another city. Khan was aware that severing Barclay's cooperation would hamper but not stop the investigations. Though averse to bloodshed, Khan decided to have the two meddlesome investigators eliminated. Their deaths were imperative for the safety and future of Womb. Rahim reported that he was unable to trace the two boys. Rahim concentrated his efforts on kidnapping Harvey and Morrison.

Rahim placed the government guest house on twenty four seven watch. He wanted to learn of their routine. The guest house stood in the centre of a large compound, surrounded by a high wall. The main gate opened onto a relatively secluded road. The two sleuths were always accompanied by armed guards. It was a setback. In the early hours of the morning, they saw a police car pull out of the gate. The police car was closely followed by the car carrying Travers's duo. A second police car followed them. Suddenly the two car convoy stopped. The armed guards formed a cordon round their charges. The bonnet of the car opened. The attention of everyone was focused on repairs. It opened a narrow window of opportunity. Rahim formulated a fool proof plan to abduct the pair. As he was about to put his plan into action, a cyclist showed up on a bicycle. He was Khan's odd job man. He informed Rahim that Khan him to arrive at the mosque immediately. The early hour aroused Rahim's suspicions. Khan never left his house so early in the morning? He feared the worst. For Rahim, Khan stood above all else. He aborted his plan and rushed to the mosque.

****

Rahim headed straight for the private chamber of the evil imam. He was more than a little apprehensive. Khan and the evil imam had been at loggerheads since Khan took possession of the statue. The imam was a vindictive man. Rahim knocked and waited for the evil imam's permission to enter. Both men looked worried. Khan came straight to the point. He said the organisation urgently needed funds. He ordered Rahim to start the collecting public donations immediately. Rahim argued that normally, funds were collected around Id and Diwali. He opined that the time was not right. With independence and partition looming closer, the Hindus would be reluctant to dole out money for a Muslim cause. Khan conceded Rahim was right. But desperate situations demand desperate action. Rahim left the imam's chamber, heavily burdened. To make matters worse he ran into the cleric. The cleric questioned Rahim's early morning visit. Rahim said that the imam wanted the two of them to collect funds from the Hindus. The cleric turned ashen. He believed the

Hindus were out to get him. 'Are you bloody mad? They turn rabid at the very sight of me.' He refused to obey the imam's directive. Rahim enjoyed watching the cleric close to hysteria. But circumstances demanded he end the charade.

CHAPTER 19

Harvey and Morrison arrived at the market square in search of Gautam and Ali. Two junior police officers accompanied them. The sheer number of hotels, guest houses and lodges was overwhelming. They split up in pairs, with a junior officer accompanying each of them. By lunch time, they had hardly managed to visit a quarter of the establishments. Morrison's partner spotted two of the evil imam's men. The men just stood around observing pedestrians go by. Morrison had misgivings about their presence. He worried that they too were here in search of the boys. He kept a sharp look out for his partner. Harvey must be told about the unexpected development. While Morrison waited for Harvey, his assistant scanned the marketplace for more members of the mosque. They stopped at a tea stall for much needed refreshment. Morrison suffered the hot sugary syrup without complaining. The officer seemed to relish the brew.

The stall offered a view most of the marketplace. A convoy of trucks led by an Austin van sped through the crowds. They ignored traffic rules and parked their vehicles as and where they liked. Morrison recognised the van. He saw the muscle man step out of the van and sweep the marketplace with his eyes. Morrison suspected sinister intent. Men armed to the teeth with sticks and swords jumped out of the trucks. They split up in groups and spread out in all directions. They appeared to target the commercial establishments. Morrison watched the muscleman cross the street with a sense of purpose. Finally Harvey joined them. Morrison drew Harvey's attention muscleman.

****

Most of the establishments in the marketplace belonged to Hindus. The decision to partition India had riled them. Rahim anticipated stubborn resistance if not worse. He headed straight for the jewellery shop of Ganga Prasad. He was the richest and the most respected shop owner. Rahim assumed that if he could persuade Prasad the rest of the community would not pose much of a problem. Besides, Prasad feared him. 'You are no longer welcome here' Prasad said even before Rahim placed a foot in the shop. Rahim returned Ganga Prasad's belligerent welcome with a threatening glare. 'I want one thousand rupees and I want it now.' Ganga Prasad's look of loathing and defiance turned to rage. The amount was five times the amount he usually donated. It was the spark that ignited the bomb. 'Have you buggers no shame. We gifted you a part of our mother land. Consider it a donation from us. Now you want our money too' Prasad shouted. Rahim overlooked the insults to his religion, community and him. In a fit of rage, Rahim grabbed Prasad by the throat and pinned him against the wall. 'I have not come here for a lecture in Indian history. I am here to collect money, and by Allah, I will have it.'

Prasad's hysterical squeal carried onto the street. A crowd of incensed Hindu, Sikh and Sindhi shop owners gathered outside the shop. They were all armed with sticks and knives. Soon they were joined by members of the general public. The crowd appeared dangerously agitated. Ganga Prasad gave a short stirring speech, inciting the crowd to retaliate. Rahim fired two shots in the air to disperse the infuriated mob. He exited the shop, keeping the mob at bay with his gun.

In minutes the marketplace turned into a battleground. A band of Muslims made a beeline for the jewellery shop. A Hindu contingent rushed to confront them. The adversaries met in the centre. Stones, bricks and soda bottles rained down on the square. The Hindu rioters ravaged Muslim businesses. The Muslims set Hindu shops alight. Molotov cocktails replaced less lethal missiles. Men on both sides fell dead or severely wounded. Rahim charged through the madness towards the van. He feared being arrested by the police. In police records he was a wanted criminal. Khan's influence had kept them at bay. Rahim ducked and weaved to avoid flying missiles. He hurdled over fallen bodies and scattered debris. In the midst of the madness Rahim saw Harvey and Morrison run into a by lane. Momentarily he vacillated over pursuing the Englishmen. He recalled that they posed a very real threat to Womb. He threw caution to the wind and decided to apprehend them. Rahim knew the by-lane ended at the railway station. He knew of a shorter route that would enable him to intercept the two Englishmen at the station. He gathered a few of his men and told them to follow the two Englishman into the by-lane. Rahim and one of his men ran down the shortcut.

CHAPTER 20

Morrison, Harvey and the junior police officers were trapped in the raging madness. All around them people were being killed or maimed and shops set ablaze. They rushed into a nearby Hindu restaurant. The owner was in the process of downing the shutters. The sight of two Englishmen in his establishment sent him into a state of panic. He knew the Hindu rioters would show no mercy if they saw the Englishmen. The owner begged them to leave. He explained he wanted to close shop and return home before the rioters spotted them. Morrison understood the hotelier's untenable situation. Harvey refused to leave. A heated argument broke out between the two. Morrison managed to pacify his partner. Warily they stepped into the midst of the chaos. Lethal objects flew past within inches of them. Seeing Englishmen in their midst, hard core Hindus pelted them with bricks and stones. A brick struck one of the junior officer's, face. The officer reeled but bore the pain with fortitude. Morrison and Harvey retaliated by firing shots in the air. Morrison suggested they take refuge in a cul-de-sac that was free of conflict. Harvey regarded cul-de-sacs as death traps. He vehemently rejected the suggestion. They noticed men, women and children rushing into a parallel lane. They fought their way through the fracas and followed them. A band of irate rioters gave chase. It was plain to see that they had mayhem on their minds. Harvey noticed that the mob was leaderless and clueless of a viable strategy. They formed a defensive cordon around the vulnerable civilians. When the horde came within range, they opened fire. Despite the casualties, the horde continued to advance. Without warning, the junior officers downed their weapons. They flatly refused to train their guns on their Hindu brethren. A Muslim gang followed the Hindus into the lane. They were far more organised. A vicious battle erupted between the two factions. The junior officers joined the battle to assist the Hindu contingent. The battle between the two factions offered Morrison the opportunity to herd the civilians to safety. They arrived at an intersection. A narrow dirt road branched off the lane. The dirt road connected to a parallel road at the other end. The dirt road was uninhabited and peaceful. To the west, the parallel led to the station. They advised the civilians to hurry to safety. They waited till the civilians were out of sight. It was heart-warming to see the two communities unite in their moment of strife. Harvey and Morrison decided to avoid the station. They feared the presence of more riotous elements.

Harvey and Morrison headed east and found themselves in a deserted suburban town. The occurrence of persistent tremors had urged the residents to flee. About a dozen large and small houses lined the road. They all appeared to be abandoned. Harvey regarded abandoned townships as death traps. They were the perfect place for an ambush. He scrutinised each house for signs of occupation. Morrison regarded it as a possible haven. Faint echoes of the conflict drifted over the air. An open plot of untended land lay to the left of them. A crumbling single storied house stood to the right of them. They silently entered the derelict house through a broken window. The floor was littered with pealing plaster. They checked the ground floor rooms and proceeded up the stairs. Harvey led the way like a cat burglar and stopped to listen for signs of occupancy. Fed up with his partner's theatrics, Morrison pushed past him and entered the room. A man wielding an iron rod stood in his way. Morrison wasn't worried. The man had the physique of a witch's broom. Before Morrison could retaliate, another man pressed a knife in the nape of his neck. Harvey entered as silent as a ghost and sprang on the knife wielder like a leopard. He grabbed the hand, twisted it away from Morrison's neck and punched the man twice in the kidneys. He spun around and slammed the heel of his shoe on the broom's jaw. The broom passed out cold. They gaged and locked the muggers in an adjacent room.

Human voices drifted in from the road. They wondered if more of the knife wielder's gang had arrived. The distinct sound of men racing up the steps echoed in the stairwell. Harvey and Morrison moved to the darkest corner of the room. Four armed men entered. They looked around, puzzled by the absence of their colleagues. For one brief moment the leader's and Morrison's eyes locked. Undeterred by the gun in Morrison's hand, the man let out a high pitched scream; sprang high in the air and catapulted both feet into Morrison's chest. Morrison flew across the room and lay there unconscious. Then the high jumper spotted Harvey. He repeated the dropkick. Harvey stepped aside, grabbed both ankles, swung him through the air and slammed his head against the wall. The sound of splintering bone was unmistakable. The leader landed on the floor a tangled mass of arms and legs. The others entered the fray. One of the men reached for something under his jacket. Harvey feared it was a gun. He dived to the floor; rolled towards Morrison's fallen gun and emptied four bullets in the man's chest. The remaining two men flew down the stairs two steps at a time. Harvey slapped Morrison back to consciousness. Exhausted from all the exertion, they decided to rest for a while. Morrison insisted they move to the ground floor in the event they needed to escape. They watched the empty road through the broken window. Two men appeared on the road. They were the muscleman and a comrade. Harvey and Morrison stepped away from the window. When they peeped again, both men were gone. The disappearance made them wary. They listened for signs of entry into the compound. To their relief, all was quiet. They decided to spend the night in the house.

CHAPTER 21

The encounter with the blood thirsty monster and the apparition had shaken Gautam and Ali to the core. Ali had encountered monstrous villains before, but none compared with the murderous monster. They were wary to step out. Gautam brooded over the apparition's prediction that he and Ali would be parted. After careful deliberations, they decided to risk stepping out of the hotel. Ali warned Gautam against mindlessly straying. At the hotel entrance, Ali scanned every inch of the square for the merest indication of danger. A familiar face sipping a cup of tea caught his attention. Morrison's presence in a marketplace seemed odd. A frenzied cry of protest diverted his attention. A short podgy man was wagging a threatening finger at the muscleman. The sight amused Gautam. Suddenly a large crowd gathered outside the jewellery shop. The crowd appeared agitated. It made Ali uncomfortable. He knew that agitated crowds were capable of erupting like volcanoes. The tension around the shop was palpable. The muscleman fired two shots in the air and leapt out of the shop. Ali followed the muscleman's flight across the square with his eyes. The muscleman stopped to confer with a group of men. The presence of Morrison and the muscleman was too much of a coincidence. He decided to retreat into the safety of the hotel. He turned and saw the monster appear on the scene in the company of four others. The sight drained the blood from Ali's face. Without warning, all hell broke loose in the square. The panicked crowd stampeded in every direction. The sight of the monster forced the boys to head away from the hotel. He decided to find a way out of the marketplace. He guided Gautam towards Morrison. But the centre of the square had turned into a battlefield. Ali chose a more circuitous route. When they finally reached the tea stall, Morrison and his companion were nowhere in sight. The mayhem was spreading in their direction. Ali searched for an escape route. The hotel resembled a medieval castle with war raging at its entrance. It was unapproachable. Ali noticed family after family rush into a narrow lane. They decided to follow the families. A number of bodies lay lifeless on the ground. Fresh pools of blood around them indicated that the massacre was fairly recent. Heart rending moans and groans of the injured filled the air. The sight and sounds depressed Gautam. He insisted they stop and help the wounded. Ali grabbed Gautam by the nape of his neck and dragged him away like an angry parent would a disobedient child. They arrived at an abandoned dirt road. At the far end they could see a group of men and women. Gautam recognised the two Englishmen. They were peering round a corner like two kids engaged in a game of hide and seek. The rest of the group soon disappeared out of sight. Ali and Gautam hurried towards the junction in the hope of catching up with the man who had saved their lives. They arrived at the parallel road only to find the Englishmen were nowhere in sight. To the right the road led to a congested area. To the left the road was still, silent and empty. Ali opted for the lonely stretch of road. They entered the abandoned township. Gautam feared they were in the domain of the dead. He believed that abandoned places were always haunted. The sight of the crumbling single storied building confirmed his fears. Ali gauged it as the perfect place to hide. They were forced to make a quick decision. They saw two men approaching in the distance. Ali pulled Gautam into the tall grass of the open plot. They watched as the muscleman and a colleague passed by.

The cleric's band of bullies arrived at the marketplace when the battle was at its peak. The monster spotted the boys entering a lane. He gestured to his colleagues to follow. The commander and the monster took the road that passed through the abandoned township. The monster was in high spirits. Some distance ahead they saw Rahim and his colleague. The commander decided to wait till the two were out of sight.

CHAPTER 22

Rahim and his colleague waited at the confluence of the dirt road. Neither his men nor the Englishmen were to be seen. Rahim decided to head for the station on the chance that they were there. Rahim searched the station and the surrounding area. It seemed the Englishmen and his men had mysteriously disappeared. He figured that the abandoned township was worth a second visit. They returned to the township. He dismissed the open plot as a place the Englishmen would hide. The dilapidated structure seemed a more likely place. They saw the commander and the giant walk towards them.

Rahim and the commander started to plan their next move. A loud sneeze emitted from the open plot. The commander believed some school kids were playing truant. Rahim crept towards the sound as silent as a panther. In one swift swoop, he picked Gautam up by his collar neck and pinned Ali under his foot. He warned them to remain silent. The boys obeyed without a murmur. The giant was straining at the bit to get his hands on them.

Rahim left one man in charge of the boys. He entered the dilapidated house with the commander and the giant. They stopped just inside the entrance and scanned the area. They checked the lower floor and the backyard. Rahim indicated to the giant to check the upper floor. The giant climbed the stone steps as silently as his bulk would permit. His foot slipped on lose rubble, causing a landslide of debris. The door to the upper floor stood open. The giant charged into the room like an enraged elephant. Harvey and Morrison deftly sprang aside.

The enraged elephant slammed into the opposite wall like a runaway train. A shower of plaster rained down on the giant. He looked like a snow covered Christmas tree. Harvey knew that physical violence against the monster was futile. He let lose two bullets in the giant's back. The massive body arched backwards and crashed to the floor. The derelict shook like it had been hit by a category five earthquake. They descended one careful step at a time. They peered into the hallway. It stood silent and empty. Harvey signalled to Morrison to sprint to the front door.

The commander peppered the detective with a barrage of bullets. Harvey rolled silently onto the hallway floor and shot the commander. He heard footstep behind him. He rolled onto his back and fired blindly in the general direction. Rahim dived to the floor. His assailant was on his feet ready to shoot. But the weapon had jammed. Rahim refrained from killing his opponent. Khan needed to interrogate him. The man threw his weapon on the floor as a gesture of surrender. Rahim lowered his gun. Harvey engaged Rahim in conversation and inched closer. But that was as far as Harvey got. The hallway reverberated with gunfire. Harvey collapsed to the floor. The incident took Rahim by surprise. He saw three silhouettes against a background of bright daylight. He recognised the boys and their minder standing at the entrance.

Gautam believed they were the next to be executed. He hoped they would kill him first. He grabbed Ali's hand for courage and confidence. Rahim marched the boys to the van. The square was empty and silent. Stones, sticks, broken bottles and a myriad of other items littered the square. As Khan was away, the mosque was the only place where he could keep them. He needed to enter without the evil imam and the insane cleric's knowledge.

CHAPTER 23

Rahim entered the mosque with the boys in tow. The congregation hall lay silent and empty. He guided the boys down a corridor and into a neglected back yard. The boys were incarcerated in a dilapidated storage shed. Rahim was grateful for the absence of the evil imam and the crazy cleric. Suddenly a screeching voice pierced the silence. The voice enquired about the Englishmen. Rahim ignored the cleric. The snub sent the cleric into a fit of uncontrollable rage. He believed that Rahim had deliberately disregarded his order. He accused Rahim of plotting against him. He ordered Rahim to leave the boys in his charge. Rahim flatly refused. That was the last straw. The cleric went off to fetch the evil imam.

The cleric returned with the evil imam and five of the imam's henchmen. Gautam thought the cleric resembled a zombie. The man's skin was pale pasty. His gait was reminiscent of a Marabou Stalk. The evil imam ordered his lackeys to tie the prisoners. Rahim had no choice but to intervene. He warned the men they would need to go past him. The imam's men froze in their strides. The boys looked on with bated breath. The imam ended the stalemate with the suggestion that Rahim permit him to interrogate the boys. 'Who are you; where have you come from and why are you in Lahore? Ali nearly blundered by introducing Gautam by his real name. He stopped in time and called him Gulam. He then repeated the tall tale of his carpenter uncle. The imam was clearly unconvinced. He signalled to one of his lackeys to rough up the boys.

Rahim had detected hesitation in Ali's replies. He decided to stand by and observe the proceedings. He warned the lackey not to cause harm. The lackey stepped back. He was not prepared to defy the muscleman. Rahim decided to apply a bit of controlled aggression to get to the truth. He slapped Ali hard enough to shake his confidence. The unexpected assault surprised Ali. His rage overrode his initial fear of the muscleman. However common sense prevailed in the nick of time. Rahim had expected a defiant response. The unwarranted assault jerked Gautam out of his trance. He flew at Rahim like a peregrine falcon defending its brood. The fact that his opponent's forearm was nearly as thick as his chest did not deter the falcon. 'Just because God has endowed you with an impressive collection of muscles, does not give you the right to use your brawn against minors half your size? It is cowardly and repugnant. One can expect such behaviour from the likes of them' he said, pointing to the cleric and his men. 'Are you completely devoid of any sense of fair play? Have you no shame? How dare you hit him? What right or reason do you have to hit him? Come on, hit me. Let the world see what a coward and bully you really are.' The outburst stunned everybody in the room. Ali looked on with a sinking feeling. He committed his soul to Gautam's Goddess. To Ali's surprise the muscleman smiled at the mouse with a heart of a lion. Rahim took a moment to weigh the response. The diminutive lion heart had shown courage and loyalty. They were qualities Rahim admired and respected. The puny little fellow had won him over. The imam, the cleric and the men left, frustrated. Rahim remained with the boys. He questioned them about the reason they came to Lahore. Gautam could not contain himself any longer. He admitted Ali's story was not true.

He related his life story. Rahim was stunned. He could scarcely believe a child so young had suffered so much. However one point needed clarification. 'What is your real name?' Gautam blurted out his name without thinking. Gautam froze, knowing he had blundered. Blood drained from Ali's face. Rahim said Ali did the right thing. There was no telling what the imam would have done had he learnt of Gautam's Hindu lineage. Rahim stepped out of the shed and closed the door behind him. He decided to give the boys a chance to escape. He walked away from the shed without locking the door.

CHAPTER 24

Ali waited to hear the sound of the lock. He was surprised by the absence of any sound. He realised the muscleman had not locked the door. It was an open invitation to escape. He opened it an inch at a time, fearing it could be a trap. The backyard stood silent and empty. They scurried across the yard and peered into the passageway. It stretched out silent and inviting. They tiptoed towards the main hall. It was devoid of occupants. Ali's heart pounded like a jungle drum. He feared someone could appear at any time. At the far end the main entrance stood partially open. Ali decided to chance their luck. They stepped into the hall like two petty thieves. A faint sound of shuffling feet stopped them in their strides. They retreated to the safety of the passage. The evil imam shuffled across the hall and stopped by a tall narrow cupboard. He only needed to turn his head to see them. The imam rifled through the contents of the cupboard and withdrew a thick tome. He turned towards them, but his eyes remained glued on the book. He doddered away at a painfully slow pace. As soon as the imam was out of sight, the boys scurried to the entrance. The partially open entrance offered a glimpse of the world outside. Passing pedestrians seemed preoccupied. Cars, busses and Lorries sped by, tooting their squeaky horns. A stray dog lay by the entrance, enjoying an afternoon siesta. A vendor had set up shop next to the mutt. The vendor and the dog paid them little heed. Ali spotted the imam's fuzzy haired bodyguard and four others on the opposite side of the road. They were lost in deep conversation. None of them noticed two boys exit the mosque. Ali was bent on reaching the banyan tree lane. It was the only way he knew to the marketplace. They walked in its direction and stopped opposite the lane. A fairly large crowd of pedestrians joined them to cross the road. The flow of traffic thinned, giving the crowd the chance to cross. The entire group of pedestrians hurried in unison to the middle of the road. The relentless flow of traffic prevented them from crossing any further. Two restless teenagers chanced a crossing, causing a pile up. A Lorry driver was forced to brake hard. Cars behind the Lorry piled into one another. The Lorry driver jumped out and manhandled one of the jaywalkers. The second jaywalker attacked the driver. Every waif, vendor and passers-by regarded it as free entertainment. They jeered and clapped. The road teetered on the verge of chaos. The boys seized the opportunity to reach the lane. The pandemonium drew the attention of fuzzy hair, the evil imam's right hand man. They decided to investigate. Fuzzy hair saw the boys enter the banyan tree lane. He chased after them. The impenetrable crowd of onlookers forced him to give up the chase.

CHAPTER 25

Fuzzy hair realised he was in a sea of trouble. The evil imam would skin him alive for letting the boys escape. They returned to the mosque and examined the shed. It was empty. He was mystified. The lock was unbroken. The bars of the windows were intact. He suspected that the boys had been deliberately set free.

The evil imam had left strict orders not to be disturbed. It offered a couple of hours of reprieve. As luck would have it, they bumped into the cleric. He sensed something was amiss and questioned them. It was worse than facing the imam. He persistently insisted on knowing the cause of their problem. One of the men stuttered that the boys were missing. The cleric gaped uncomprehending. He wondered how four able bodied men could not keep two adolescent boys in a locked shed. He advised them to join a circus. In frustration he marched into the imam's chamber. The imam was incensed. He gave fuzzy hair a piece of his mind and ordered him to find the boys. The cleric asked where he proposed to begin his search. Fuzzy hair was stumped. The imam ordered fuzzy hair to either find them, or never return to the mosque.

CHAPTER 26

On Khan's return, Rahim informed him of all that had occurred. The death of the Englishmen was relief. Rahim's assistance in letting the boys escape worried him. Khan was keen to learn of the connection between the Hindu boy and the statue. A phone call from the mosque informed Khan that the evil imam had dispatched his men to find the boys. Khan and Rahim feared for their lives. It was imperative they find the boys before the imam's blood thirsty horde. Khan ordered Rahim to race to the mosque and intercept the search party.

On entering the mosque, Rahim heard the evil imam shout out instructions to the search party. He ordered them to kill the boys if necessary. Rahim stepped up and volunteered to head the team. The imam realised that Rahim was the best man for the job. He reluctantly agreed. The cleric stopped fuzzy hair on his way out. He instructed him to get hold of the boys before Rahim.

Rahim started by making enquiries at hotels and guest houses in the marketplace. He ordered fuzzy hair stay with him at all times. The man was a psychopath. The Hindu migration had commenced. The sheer numbers congested the marketplace. They were all burdened with heavy luggage; aged and ailing relatives and boisterous children. The vehicular traffic had come to a standstill. Rahim was overwhelmed by the crowds. He suspected the boys might attempt to leave Lahore. Rahim's men watched intently for any sign of their quarry. Rahim had the advantage of knowing the lay of the land. He recalled a number of narrow alleyways branching out of the road. They all meandered through congested neighbourhoods but ended up at the station. He knew Ali was street smart. He might have taken advantage of the alleyways. As a Muslim, Rahim was reluctant to force his way through the crowd of Hindus. It could incite violence. He and fuzzy hair respectfully excused their way to reach the alleyways. He sent the rest of the men to scour the station.

CHAPTER 27

Ali and Gautam engaged a hand pulled rickshaw to reach the marketplace. Gautam fell into conversation with the rickshaw driver. They discussed a plethora of topics. Ali dwelled on the chances of their survival. When they arrived at the marketplace, it was chock-a block with people. An endless stream of men, women and children inched towards the station. There was a sense of apprehension and resignation on everyone's faces. Ali and Gautam were carried forward by the crowd. The sheer numbers made Ali apprehensive. He feared running into the imam's men. Reaching the hotel was impossible. Ali steered Gautam into a lane, believing it was the same one they had taken earlier. He soon realised it was a different lane. Nothing around them looked familiar. They were apparently in a neighbourhood of the wealthy. Neatly painted walls bordered the lane. Palatial bungalows stood handsomely in the estates. The lane stood empty and quiet. The eerie silence gripped Gautam's imagination. He believed they had stepped through a time warp.

Four men entered the far end of the lane. Ali searched for a place to hide. He noticed more men approaching from the other end. Ali effortlessly scaled a ten feet high wall and pulled Gautam up behind him. A row of hedges ran the full length of the compound. The hedges bordered an immaculately manicured lawn. A flagstone walkway separated the boundary wall and the hedges. They hid behind the hedges. Tense moments ticked by. The silence was broken by someone calling out to the residents. Ali peered over the hedge. The caller was the muscleman. A man and a dog emerged from the mansion. The man confronted

Rahim in a distinctly unfriendly manner. The dog too seemed unhappy about the unwarranted disturbance. He made his displeasure known with growls and barks. Ali heard Rahim say that they were tourists and requested for some water and permission to rest a short while on the lawn. The man acceded to their request. Rahim entered the gate followed by fuzzy hair and the rest. The dog was having none of it. He charged at them like a demon from hell. The dog was not Rahim's only problem. A shrill cry like that of an angry banshee pierced the peace. It emitted from the vicinity of the house. A middle aged lady, shaped like a beach ball, rolled purposefully across the lawn. Her demeanour was undeniably confrontational. The beach ball ordered the intruders off her property. Rahim repeated his lost tourist story but received no sympathy. They left like obedient schoolchildren.

Ali decided it was time for them to leave. The beach ball appeared to be an unfriendly woman. They crawled on all fours towards the gate. A few feet away a hedge started to growl. Gautam jumped like a startled grasshopper and landed close to Ali. He had heard tales of whispering grass, singing sands, walking banyan trees, but never growling hedges. A snout appeared through the bush, followed by a large black head with bared canines. Ali tried to pacify the dog with chirrups and finger clicks. The mutt responded with threatening growls. He was bent on seeing the strangers off his property. Ali knew that if they ran, it would awaken the mutt's primeval instinct to give chase. He pelted the creature with pebbles. The dog responded with a mock charge. A shrill cry pierced the air. The dog seemed torn between duty and obedience. Exasperated, she called the dog again, hitting a high soprano note. The dog retreated with his tail in his grove. Ali seized the opportunity to leave. They approached the gate on all fours. The final few feet to the gate offered them no cover. Ali told Gautam to run like he was being pursued by the giant. The sight of the dog running towards them gave Gautam a much need boost. They were out of the gate like a pair of jackrabbits.

Gautam and Ali headed in the direction away from the marketplace. They ended in a crowded vegetable market. A deafening train whistle in the immediate vicinity indicated the proximity of the station. Ali kept a sharp look out for Rahim and his men. An irate old man captured everyone's attention. He vented his pent up emotions by lambasting the Muslims and the British. The boys continued their annoyingly slow progress towards the station. Finally they entered the station. Ali spotted Rahim at the platform gate. The muscleman closely watched the passing procession. A group of Muslim teenagers were taunting the migrating Hindus. Overcome with emotion, the Hindus retaliated. The station turned into a raging battlefield. Ali noticed that Rahim's attention had shifted to the skirmish. Taking advantage of the moment, they charged through the gate.

****

Rahim ordered fuzzy hair and others to survey the platforms. He climbed onto a platform bench to get an Ariel view. He spotted Ali and Gautam among the commuters. A tug on his trousers diverted Rahim's attention. He looked down into tear filled eyes of a terrified girl. He lifted the girl on his shoulders and told her to spot her parents. After many anxious moments, the child hysterically called out to her mother. The distraction caused Rahim to lose sight of the boys. He resumed his search with greater determination. He surveyed the platform again by standing on top of a stack of crates. An indignant lady was scolding Gautam for some reason. He kept his eyes fixed on the spot. But he was unable to dismount. The crowds had encircled him. Disregarding the crowd, he managed to dismount and elbow his way towards the screaming lady.

Ali turned to see the muscleman towering above the crowd. He pushed Gautam towards the waiting train. The loudspeakers announced the train's departure. The train's whistle pierced the air. Ali pushed Gautam through the crowd towards the train. The train jerked forward and the wheels started to roll. Ali summoned all his strength and threw Gautam into the carriage door. Ali's attempt to follow was thwarted by a vice like grip on his shirt collar. The train gained momentum and left the station with Gautam on board. Ali watched the train move away. He looked on with bated breath as Gautam struggled to enter the carriage. Tears welled in his eyes. Rahim held on to his prisoner. He noticed Ali glaring at him with intense hate wild rage. He could understand the boy's pain and anger. Seeing Ali's emotional turmoil brought out the gentler side of Rahim. He placed a hand on Ali's shoulder and reminded him that everybody loses a loved one at some time. Rahim drove his captive to Khan's mansion.

BOOK 3

CHAPTER 1

Rahim introduced Ali to Khan. Ali answered all of Khan's questions in monosyllables. His thoughts concentrated on ways to kill everyone in the mosque. Out of the blue, the cleric showed up. Anticipating an assault from Ali, Rahim stood between Ali and the uninvited guest. The cleric wasted no time in disparaging the lad. 'Well, well, well, is it the sodomite I see before me? Where is your little sex toy?' Ali was unable to control his anger. He lunged forward and proceeded to choke the life out of the cleric. Rahim was forced use all his strength to extricate the cleric from the boy's grip. Khan ordered Rahim to release the boy. He dismissed the cleric with a wave of his hand. After a bit of gentle coaxing, Ali opened up. He related his life story. He told of a rich man who offered him a job in his house. However he expected sexual favours in return. Having nowhere to go and no one to turn to, Ali suffered the indignity for a number of years. One day the man summoned Ali to his room. When Ali entered, the man was lying motionless on his bed. Ali realised the man was dead. He found thirty seven rupees on the bedside table. He decamped with the loot. Khan and Rahim looked on in stunned silence. They were overwhelmed by the narrative. Both men were aware that the imam would move heaven and earth to get his hands on the boy. They decided to transfer him to offered accommodation in the mansion.

The dismissal enraged the cleric. He marched out of the office, slamming the door behind him. The cleric went directly to the evil imam's chamber. He trembled with uncontrollable rage. He reported the incident in graphic detail. The imam was slighted by Khan's high handedness. He gave Khan a piece of his mind over the phone. Khan responded by forbidding the cleric from entering the mansion ever again.

The cleric had connections in the mansion to circumvent Khan's orders. Late in the night Ali's room door flew open. The cleric and fuzzy hair barged in. Fuzzy hair was visibly uncomfortable. He feared retribution from Rahim. The cleric warned Ali that Khan and Rahim could not protect him. The imam was all powerful. He questioned Ali about the reason for his and Gautam's visit to Lahore. He cautioned Ali not to repeat the cock and bull story about his carpenter uncle. Ali did not respond. He just stood and stared at the intruders. He was consumed with hate and anger. The cleric threw insults at him. Ali lost control when the cleric passed a snide remark about Gautam's sexuality. He lunged at the cleric and knocked him to the floor. He placed a foot on the cleric's throat and started apply pressure. The terrified cleric struggled under the pressure. Fuzzy hair punched Ali in the face, sending him crashing to the floor. Ali was down but not out. He stood up and wiped his bleeding lip. The bodyguard seized Ali by the collar and shook him like a ragdoll. A soft but authoritative voice brought the matter to an end. Khan entered with a bodyguard. He incarcerated the cleric and fuzzy hair in a potting shed. The following morning the imam phoned Khan. He demanded that the two men be set free and Ali handed over to him.

****

The following night Ali found three men standing in the doorway. Muscles rippled through their skin-fitting T-Shirts. They had murder on their minds. Ali snatched a bottle of water and threw it at them. The bottle hit one of them. He grabbed his trouser belt and approached, swinging the heavy brass buckle.

Ali knew this was a battle he could not win. There was only one way out. He screamed at the top of his voice. The ear piercing scream unsettled the intruders. They were clearly at sixes and sevens. Ali's buckle hit one on the temple and the other on the jaw. The scream brought the security guards rushing to Ali's room. Khan knew the imam was persistent. He would not rest till he had Ali in his clutches. He sent for Rahim. They decided to send Ali to the training camp as soon as possible.

****

The following day Rahim entered Ali's room looking downcast. He sat next to Ali, struggling for words. There was no gentle way to break the news. Rahim said that the train carrying Gautam had met with a terrible accident. As per the information they had, there were no survivors. Rahim watched helplessly as Ali sat frozen to the spot, staring fixedly at nothing. Tears rolled down his cheeks. Pangs of guilt gnawed at Ali's conscience. Had he made a more concerted effort to board the train, he would have died with his friend. He buried his face in his hands and wept uncontrollably. Finally the tears dried up. Through clenched teeth he muttered 'The imam, the cleric and the others are all going to die slow painful deaths.' He recalled Gautam saying that life is like a book. The past constitutes the chapters one has already read. The future is hidden in the pages that follow. No matter how distressing or depressing the tale may be, one must continue to pursue the story to the very end. He felt sapped of all physical and emotional strength. A note arrived addressed to Ali. It read, you see what happens to infidels who desecrate Allah's sanctum. Ali leapt off his bed and retrieved his knife from his bag. He told Rahim to make preparations for the cleric's funeral. Rahim had to use force to restrain his incensed charge.

CHAPTER 2

Gautam clung on to the assistance bar for all he was worth. His right leg rested on the floorboard, while the left dangled in the air. The motion of the train flung him inward and out with every turn of the wheel. A group of good Samaritans risked their lives to save the boy. He repeatedly thanked his stout hearted saviours. Gautam realised that Ali was missing. He anxiously called out his name. Soon his anxiety turned to panic. He made several attempts to jump off the train. Finally he accepted the painful reality. He sank to the floor and wept. An elderly man named Shivastrava took charge of Gautam. Gautam narrated his life story through sobs and sniffles. The old man placed a gentle hand on his shoulder. He reminded Gautam that there was not a man on the train who hadn't lost a loved one. The old man related his own tale of woe. He had watched his entire family butchered by hooligans. For reasons known only to God, he and his granddaughter Padmini escaped with their lives. Shivastrava introduced him to a girl roughly Gautam's age.

The train raced through the night, carrying its load of depressed passengers. Sporadic conversations were carried out in hushed tones. Gautam's thoughts focused on Ali. Shivastrava snored while Padmini watched the darkness whizz by. A moonbeam washed over her face, accentuating her alluring features. Gautam found it hard to avert his gaze. A strange warm feeling flooded his heart. He felt a curious tingle in his crotch. The feeling was unknown to him. Gautam hesitantly stretched his arm, like one attempting to pet a vicious dog and touched her hand. The girl turned and smiled at him. The moment of puppy love soon passed.

Suddenly the carriage shook like it was hit by an earthquake. It overturned and skidded forward several hundred feet. Passengers were thrown every which way. A part of the carriage roof was sheared clean off its moorings. Dead and dismembered bodies were strewn all around. Rivulets of blood meandered past limbless and decapitated torsos. Moans of pain and pleas for help filled the air. Gautam rose unsteadily and checked for injuries. He had suffered painful cuts and bruises all over his body. Padmini suffered only a few lacerations. Shivastrava lay senseless on the floor, with his body pressed against the bulkhead. A deep gash ran from his hairline to his cheekbone. Blood covered his face. Gautam ripped off his shirt sleeve and cleaned and dressed the man the best he could. Seventeen men, women and children scrambled out of the wrecked carriage. They stood stunned and shaken in the cold night air. Soon passengers from other compartments joined them. Sixty three people of a train load of nearly a thousand survived the mishap.

The group made their way over the uneven terrain in absolute darkness. A sharp report of gunfire pierced the night air. The rhythmic tattoo of hoof beats warned them of approaching trouble. Men and beasts with flaming torches surrounded them. A mounted marauder spoke in a loud and clear voice. He ordered them to surrender all their valuables. If the smallest trinket was found on them, they would pay with their lives. The passengers did as they were told. A teenage girl was found to hide a gold coin of lord Ganesh. She was gang raped and set alight. The sight devastated a group of elders. They hurled abuses at the marauders. They were all mercilessly butchered.

The rest resumed their journey, leaving fourteen elderly men and the charred remains of a girl behind. They rested on top of a high forested hill. The dim glow of dawn brought a collection of thatched roofs into view. The timid advised they should continue. The intrepid insisted on investigating the village. The women, children and the elderly remained on the hill. Gautam was among the intrepid. They threw caution to the wind and called out to the residents. A pack of feral dogs answered with loud barks. The mutts seemed unsure of what to make of the strangers. Finally a middle aged lady emerged from her hut. She wore a Muslim garb. She eyed them suspiciously. The youngsters related their plight and said they were in dire need of sustenance. The woman and other villagers donated whatever they could. The woman informed them that they were just twelve miles from the proposed new border. The group left the village and arrived in a town in Indian Punjab.

****

They group parted with hugs and promises to stay in touch. Gautam, Shivastrava and Padmini made their way to Shivastrava's family home in Delhi. The bungalow and the property screamed out for urgent attention. The travel fatigued trio waited patiently at the front gate for the housekeeper to appear. After what seemed an eternity, a man stumbled and swayed his way towards them. In his inebriated state he ordered them off the property. Shivastrava gave him a piece of his mind. The housekeeper squealed with joy when at last he recognised Shivastrava. He bowed to undo his error and hit his head on the gate. He produced a bunch of keys and stared at them, like they were some modern technological marvel. Finally it dawned on him that they were a bunch of keys. Every time he attempted to open the padlock, he swayed back and forth, missing his mark. At last he threw his hands in the air in exasperation. He complained that the lock kept moving. Shivastrava clasped the housekeepers hand and directed it to the keyhole. 'Now turn' the old man ordered. The housekeeper released the key, spun around and stood with his back to the gate. Shivastrava's patience finally ran out. He asked Gautam to do the needful. After several attempts Gautam succeeded. The housekeeper hurried to the rear of the house to open the front door. Shivastrava feared they may never see the man again. A series of loud crashes from within the house indicated his housekeeper was on his way. They were greeted by a whiff of musty air; a cloud of dust and the nauseating stench of alcoholic fumes. Shivastrava was overcome with nostalgia. He reminisced about the happy times. His despondent nostalgia was interrupted by a shrill shriek. It caused Padmini and Gautam to jump out of their skins. Missus housekeeper stood in the doorway, smiling broadly. She touched Shivastrava's feet; chided her inebriated husband and rolled away to prepare lunch. The housekeeper left to sleep off his intoxication.

CHAPTER 3

Rahim drove Ali to the training camp in the middle of the night. Khan believed that neither the imam nor the cleric was aware of its existence. The camp lay close to the border with Afghanistan. It was surrounded by woods and barren land. Rahim introduced Ali to the commander in charge, his future trainer and the camp imam. Ali was taken to a cluster of tents at the north end of the camp. It would be his home sweet home for the next two years. Each cluster was managed by an instructor and a tent monitor. The monitors were selected by virtue of their seniority and combat ability. They in turn answered to an instructor. The instructors were all retired commandos from a number of different countries.

The chief commanding officer was a retired S.A.S. officer of the rank of major. The officer had converted to Islam during his sojourn in Africa. He demanded absolute obedience and respect from all. Severe retribution was the penalty for insubordination, disrespect and disregard for rules. Ali soon developed a healthy respect for the instructors. The chief commander checked each cluster once a week. This did not include surprise visits. Though he had it better than most, Ali felt like a convict. It was impossible for anyone to leave or enter the camp without being spotted. He resented the strictly imposed restrictions on his freedom. He considered running away. But that was easier said than done. On the day of his quarterly leave, he would spend time charting out the lay of the camp and its surroundings.

On Ali's first evening in the camp, his monitor called Tuglaq approached him. He was a powerfully built man. He had allocated different chores for everyone. Ali was expected to polish his shoes every evening. Ali flatly refused. The others in the tent tensed. Tuglaq could not believe his ears. He repeated his demand. Ali continued to disobey the order. Tuglaq rose and approached Ali menacingly. He intended to mortify the new trainee. Ali reminded Tuglaq that he was here to become a commando, not a cobbler. Tuglaq lashed out at Ali. Ali deftly avoided the blow. Tuglaq threw a second punch at his defiant opponent. Once again Ali dodged the wrecking ball. Ali responded with a kick that connected with the Tuglaq's crotch. The man merely winced. Ali repeated the attack but missed the mark. For one built like a bovine, Tuglaq moved like a spritely gazelle. In a fit of rage he lifted Ali and threw him across the tent. Ali hit the floor, a tangled mess of arms and legs. At that very moment the chief commanding officer entered the tent. He was annoyed at seeing Ali on the ground. He gave Tuglaq a verbal lashing. He introduced Ali to the inmates as Rahim's protégé. The very mention of Rahim's name unnerved Tuglaq.

****

A year passed by surprisingly quickly. The day of the annual competition to gauge the best trainees and monitors finally arrived. Ali and Tuglaq defeated all their rivals with ease. The two adversaries entered the ring. The spectators welcomed them with loud applause, whistles and catcalls. Tuglaq glared at his opponent with loathing. Ali was apprehensive. He doubted he would win, but he was determined to end up in one piece. The participants were warned of severe punishment in the event of foul play. Tuglaq and Ali circled one another, searching for an opportunity to attack. Driven by vengeful ire, Tuglaq charged at his opponent like a rodeo bull. Ali stepped out of the way;

stretched out his leg and tripped the bull. Tuglaq floundered, staggered and came down with an earth shaking thud. Tuglaq's admirers fell silent. Tuglaq jumped to his feet unfazed. He repeatedly attacked without strategy. His clumsy attempts drew jeers from his fans. Tuglaq was beside himself with rage. Ali's confidence grew with every failed assault. He made the mistake of losing his concentration. Tuglaq's massive bulk slammed into his chest. Ali flew through the air like a missile and fell to earth with a thud. For a brief moment he lay still, stunned and shaken. The pro-Tuglaq spectators let out a cry of cheer. But Tuglaq was not satisfied with victory. He wanted Ali to beg for mercy. The bison let out a cry of triumph and lifted his gigantic foot to slam it into Ali's face. Ali spun away and kicked out at Tuglaq's exposed groin. Instead, the toe connected with Tuglaq's patella. Tuglaq merely grunted and readied himself for a second assault. Ali sprang to his feet, ready to face a second onslaught. Tuglaq attempted to slam into Ali again. Ali countered with a drop kick. Tuglaq remained standing, but it dented his confidence. The jeers rang in his ears. He felt humiliated. Tuglaaq decided to end the fight with dignity. Tuglaq approached Ali with an extended hand of friendship. The anti-climax was met with a collective shout of disappointment from the spectators. They chanted insults at both the contestants. The two adversaries ignored the shouts and stepped out of the arena as friends.

****

The quarterly leave was an eagerly awaited occasion. The trainees insisted that the champion trainee accompany them to the club. He reluctantly agreed. It was located in a nearby hamlet. Ali refused to gamble or tipple. Once the gambling started, the booze flowed freely. Within the hour, most could hardly tell a spade from a club. They walked like they were on black ice. Their stipend of fifty rupees a month evaporated faster than exposed ether. Tempers flared at the drop of a hat. The session ended in heated arguments. Tuglaq unexpectedly visited the club. It surprised everybody. He had never once stepped into what he considered the den of evil. Tuglaq invited Ali to tea. When they returned, the gambling den was empty. Everybody had moved to another part of the club. They found the gamblers in what Tuglaq described as a place of sin. Ali watched wide eyed at the collection of sensuous girls parading past. Girls of every shape, size and hue were available for a price. They proved to be a luring temptation. A girl in her late teens riveted Ali's attention. His loins tingled with lust. He chose her to be his partner for the rest of the day.

The call girl led Ali into a room no bigger than an average sized storeroom. He could barely contain his excitement. He had not enjoyed the company of a girl for a very long time. He felt self-conscious and nervous. He wondered if he would be up to the task. The girl snuggled up to him, undressing him with one hand while caressing his hardness with the other. They lay on the mattress naked, embraced in passionate foreplay. Ali stuck his tongue down her throat; cupped her breasts and stroked her loins. They rolled over. She got on top of him and ran her tongue all the way down his body, taking his erection in her mouth. They were ready for the grand finale. Stupefied by sensual pleasure, Ali fumbled with penetration. She needed to guide his penis to the right place. It was over almost as soon as it started. Ali spilled his load before the act. He gazed at her, feeling embarrassed and inadequate. She returned his gaze, wearing an understanding smile. 'It's alright' she whispered 'it happens to almost everyone the first time. It won't take long before you're ready to go again.'

Their moment of passion was interrupted by shouting in the neighbouring room. The argument was obviously over money. The man begged and pleaded for compassion. The woman insisted she be paid immediately. She opened the door and called out to the security men. It brought a group of roughnecks racing to the room. They were armed to the teeth. They entered the room and started to beat the penniless lover. The man's moans and groans brought out Ali's spirit of comradeship. He prepared to go to the assistance of his fellow trainee. The girl tried in vain to stop him. Ali felt a blade against his neck as he entered the neighbouring room. They threatened him with dire consequences if he did not leave. Ali gripped the man's wrist and slammed his fist in his face. He followed with a kick in the groin. Blood flowed from the man's nose and lips. The man sank to the floor. The remaining four piled onto Ali. Hockey sticks and steel pipes rained down on him from all directions. Ali squatted, shielding his head with his arms and waited for the assault to end. Sooner than expected, the onslaught ended. Ali looked up to see men fly through the air and crash to the floor. Tuglaq stood over them with a defiant glare. Four more men rushed to the aid of their colleagues. Ali and Tuglaq took them on. At the end of the scuffle all the security men lay battered and bloodied. Tuglaq asked if there was anyone else who wished to settle dues with his associates. They found the penniless lover had disappeared. Ali and Tuglaq decided to pay Sheroo the proprietor a visit. They were stopped at the entrance by security staff. An argument ensued. One of the security men made the mistake of pushing Ali. It was the last thing he did that day. Tuglaq grabbed the man by the wrist; lifted him in the air from his armpit and slammed him face first onto the floor. The rest of the security men did not move a muscle. They found Sheroo pacing the floor with a whip in his hand. The defaulter was bound to a chair, bloody and bruised. The unexpected intrusion stopped Sheroo in his stride. One of the goons decided to attack. Ali butted the attacker giving him a bloody nose. Sheroo stood petrified to the spot. They settled the matter of their colleague's dues. Sheroo told them to consider it a gift from him. He watched helplessly as Tuglaq threw the colleague over his shoulder and marched out of the room. On their way out, Ali noticed men carrying crates bearing the camp logo. The men quickly disappeared into a room. Fuzzy hair was one of them.

Ali reported the matter to the commanding officer. The commander decided to investigate. He ordered the storekeeper to show him the latest inventory. The storekeeper turned pale. The commander waited while the storekeeper and his helpers sorted and counted every item. Nearly a quarter of the stock was missing. The commander had no other choice but to send Ali to apprise Rahim of the situation. A written communique could be intercepted by the wrong people. Ali was cautioned against the evil imam or the cleric learning of his arrival. Rahim and Ali arrived at the camp two days later.

CHAPTER 4

It took Gautam, Padmini, the gardener and his wife days to make the house liveable. Shivastrava faced financial problems. He considered selling the property. He considered sacking the housekeeper. However, sentimental attachments and low prices urged him procrastinate. Too many fond memories lay buried in its walls. He faced the burden of educating Padmini and Gautam. The battle between necessity and sentiments drove him to the point of despair. With no one else to turn to, Shivastrava poured out his troubles to his two teenage companions. Padmini had no suggestions. Gautam reminded him that God had steadfastly stood by them through the most difficult times. He was certain God would not abandon them now.

As weeks dragged by, their situation worsened. Winter was nearly upon them. Woollen blankets and fire wood would soon become a necessity. While Shivastrava grappled with his problems, Padmini and Gautam spent most of their time in childish pursuit. Until recently he enjoyed the kid's frolicking. Now it started to get on his nerves. To add to his burden, a mongrel pup strayed in and decided to make the old house his home. They named him Mangal. The Shivastravas and Mangal were resting in the front porch. The puppy looked towards the gate and yelped. A stranger waited at the gate. Gautam went to meet the visitor. Shivastrava was delighted to meet his cousin Laxman after nearly twenty five years. The two cousins hugged and back slapped one another. They had been best friends since they were toddlers. They were dubbed the devils of the family. They reminisced about their many childhood escapades and laughed raucously. Their conversation turned from the happy days of childhood to the trials and tribulations of the present. The cousin too had experienced personal tragedies. They discussed setting up a small partnership business. Laxman suggested a medium sized department store in the city. As a retired general manager of a bank, he could arrange a bank loan against Shivastrava's property. The two cousins shook hands and wasted no time to start the ball rolling. In a little over a year the store started to show a profit. Padmini had no trouble getting admission in a school. Gautam was considered too old to attend junior school and too young to pursue occupational training. Shivastrava engaged a private tutor. Five years of the drudgery of education coupled with fun and frolic flew past. Gautam passed a government exam that qualified him to attend college. Shivastrava used his influence to get Gautam admitted in one of the best colleges in Delhi. But Gautam was apprehensive. The tales he had heard of college life made him uncomfortable. Shy in the presence of Gautam found it difficult to make friends.

College life turned out better than Gautam expected. The girls found his youth and shyness endearing. But the boys branded him a sissy. They tended to bully him. Gautam refrained from retaliating. He befriended a boy named Ramesh who was also timid and shy. The boys called them mister and missus sissy. A rumour spread through college that Gautam was an illegitimate child of a millionaire businessman. It riled Gautam. He decided to confront his detractors. But he refrained from violence. There were too many of his detractors. Besides, his friend would be as useless in a fight, as a puppy facing a pack of wolves. Gautam decided to ignore the rumour and concentrate on his studies.

The exams were upon them. Gautam and Ramesh found a quiet corner to prepare for the geography paper. Three bullies confronted them and demanded five rupees by the end of the day. They stipulated the time and place. News of the ultimatum spread like wildfire. A crowd of students gathered to witness the outcome. One of the bullies held Gautam against a wall. The second bully inspected his pockets. Ramesh cowered in a corner petrified. Every offensive and defensive move Ali had taught him came rushing back to him. Gautam slammed his right foot on the ridge bone of the bully's foot. The bully cried out in pain and released Gautam. Gautam let loose a volley of punches. It surprised the other bullies. They were hesitant to attack. One of the more defiant bullies approached from behind. He threw his arm around Gautam neck and proceeded to choke him. Gautam slammed the back of his head on the bully's nose. He grabbed the boy's crotch and squeezed with all his might. The choker screamed and released his grip. The remaining bullies fled the scene like spooked deer.

The brawl completely altered Gautam's image. The boys approached him with respect. The girls considered him a hero. They fabricated excuses just to talk to him. But Gautam's heart and soul belonged to Padmini. The following four years were full of fun. He seemed to have forgotten his main purpose in life. The years rolled by with lightning speed. Gautam was now a graduate. Accolades rained down on him. But his most treasured reward was the secret kiss from Padmini. With a bit of influence and palm greasing Shivastrava secured a job for Gautam in the Indian Administrative Service.

CHAPTER 5

Life in the camp was not looking good for Ali. He was fed up with the monotonous religious lectures. Ali was bent on ending the mind numbing monotony. He constantly bombarded the imam with blasphemous questions and arguments. The infuriated imam banned him from attending religious classes. Ali was just as relieved as the imam. However, Ali was now burdened with the task of learning to speak, read and write English. On the field, Ali and Tuglaq were shunned by most of the inmates. The gun runners had threatened trainees and monitors not to hobnob with them. They were forced to practice on their own. At the end of the session they would have a cup of tea at the canteen. It was an open air affair under a spreading tree. Two long wooden tables and benches was the only furniture. When they arrived, two instructors were involved in a lively debate on politics. Ali lifted his cup to take a sip of the hot brew. The cup shattered in his hand. He was left holding the handle. The brew had splattered every which way. A bullet had lodged in the table top. Ali, Tuglaq and the debaters rolled off the bench. They formed a posse to search for the sniper. The group hurried into the surrounding woods. Tuglaq was convinced Sheroo was behind the assassination attempt.

Ali found a calling card in the foliage. He pocketed it without anyone noticing. The foot prints revealed the sniper was wearing regulation boots. That was insufficient proof of the sniper's identity. After an hour, they called off the search. Ali informed the commander about the boot prints. The commander ordered every inmate of the camp to assemble on the training field in full uniform. The commander inspected the troupes. He looked for anyone with muddy soles or recently cleaned boots. Trainees, as a rule, do not polish shoes until bedtime. They concluded that the sniper did not belong to the camp. The commander worried that the culprit would succeed in killing Ali if he wasn't found soon. Rahim had to be told of the incident. He secretly dispatched Ali to Lahore again. The first thing Ali did was show Rahim the calling card. Rahim recognised it as belonging to Salim the sniper. But it did not make sense. Salim would not miss a fly in full flight. He concluded that the assassin had forged Salim's card. Rahim accompanied Ali back to the camp.

A light overnight shower signalled the arrival of the monsoons. There was an uncomfortable chill in the early morning air. Rahim joined Ali and Tuglaq at the tea stall. Ali and Tuglaaq ordered mince, two chapattis and tea. A friendly mutt approached Ali, wagging its tail. Ali threw him some mince. The dog wolfed it down and started to convulse. Green coloured froth emitted from his mouth. Rahim realised the dog had been poisoned. He quickly pulled the plates and tea cups away. The unfortunate animal lay dead at Ali's feet. The incident made the commander apprehensive and angry. Rahim had the food confiscated and sent to Lahore for analysis. The commander summoned the entire tea stall staff. A waiter was found to be missing. The tea stall manager had recently employed him. He had been previously employed by Sheroo. Enquiries revealed that the guards had seen no one enter or leave the camp. Rahim decided to pay the club a visit.

The following morning Ali stepped out of his tent. A thick fog had settled on the camp and its surroundings. Ali heard the crack of a rifle and instinctively dived to the ground. Someone in the tent screamed in pain. A fellow trainee lay on the ground, bleeding profusely from his chest. His fellow trainees used their first aid knowledge to try and stem the flow. Ali sent one of the juniors to fetch the commander and the doctor and another to fetch Rahim. In minutes the cluster was swarming with trainees and seniors from neighbouring tents. Rahim, the doctor and the commander arrived on the scene a bit too late. The trainee was dead.

Rahim, Ali and Tuglaq paid the club a visit. Rahim asked a watchman to direct them to Sheroo's lair. The watchman flatly refused. Rahim locked the man's arm behind his back and twisted till the man cried out in pain. Tuglaq did his bit and kicked the entrance door open. He did the same with Sheroo's bedroom door. Sheroo rolled out of bed and reached for his gun a moment too late. Ali had his gun pointing at Sheroo's head. Rahim ordered Sheroo to assemble his entire staff in the compound. The young waiter was among them. The waiter was rough housed by Ali and Tuglaq. He eventually admitted that the poisoning had been ordered by fuzzy hair. He swore he had never heard of the evil imam. They turned their attention to Sheroo. Sheroo flatly denied any knowledge of the incident. Rahim could tell the man was telling the truth.

****

On his return to Lahore, Rahim paid Salim a visit. He informed the sniper of the attempts on Ai's life. He showed the sniper the forged calling card. Salim showed Rahim the difference between his card and the forgery. He pointed out an almost imperceptible dot next to the trigger. He said that the imam had employed an ex-student of his as a sniper. The sniper went by the name of Nishana. Nishana was a crack shot, but over anxious. Through the process of elimination, the finger of suspicion pointed directly at the evil imam. The forensic analysis of the mince indicated that the poison was extracted from a rare plant found only in the jungles of Assam. Rahim recalled that an investigation into fuzzy hair's antecedents revealed that his father worked on a tea estate in Assam. Fuzzy Hair was born and brought up on the estate. The assassination attempts had commenced soon after Ali and Tuglaq's clash with Sheroo. It meant the proprietor of the den was in some way connected to the evil imam. Rahim decided apprise Khan of the assassination attempts.

Three points about Rahim's report troubled Khan. The first, how did the imam learn of the camp? He had taken every precaution to find a secluded place. The second, what made someone choose to run a club in such a remote area? The third, how did the imam learn that Ali was stationed at the camp? Khan suspected that the evil imam had spies in the mansion. He feared for Ali's safety. He had grown quite fond of the young man. Khan decided to transfer Ali back to Lahore. Khan's solicitors learnt that the property originally belonged to the imam's maternal family. The imam's nephew Sheroo inherited the property. He got involved with a syndicate smuggling liquor across the India Pakistan border and opium from Afghanistan. Sheroo was caught and faced a seven years sentence. The imam used all his influence to get the sentence reversed. In exchange, the nephew was made to transfer the ownership of the property to the imam. A couple of years ago, the imam constructed the club and told his nephew run the business. The construction had not been registered with the district authorities. Their records showed that it is just an open plot of land.

Khan invited the evil imam to tea. The imam had a weakness for the delicious and expensive snacks usually on offer. He readily accepted. Knowing the imam's penchant for ostentation, Khan sent his Daimler, instead of the Rover. The imam made a grand entrance. Waiters plied him with a variety of canapés and choice cheeses. Khan knew the only way to get the imam to reveal his hand was to rile him. After a bit of small talk, Khan broached the topic of the property close to the Afghan border. He said that he wished to start an orphanage there. He asked the imam to donate the property. The imam fought to stay calm but he had lost all self-control. He said between clenched teeth hat it was his maternal family property. It was not for sale. Nor did he intend to donate it. Khan maintained his sangfroid. He said that someone was running a club on it. The imam flew off the handle. 'What it is used for is none of your God damn business.' The waiters came around with more snacks. The sight of smoked salmon and camembert was too much to resist. After wolfing them down, the imam bid his guest farewell and left the mansion in a huff. The meeting had revealed that the imam knew of the club. In all likelihood he had a hand in the attempted assassinations. Khan discussed the matter with Rahim. Rahim suggested they kidnap fuzzy hair and Nishana and force the truth out of them. The plan made Khan apprehensive. The imam was a formidable foe.

****

The imam returned to the mosque in a foul mood. He suspected that Khan was aware of the gun smuggling. He summoned fuzzy hair. The imam gave his bodyguard a piece of his mind and sent him packing. To avoid a chance encounter with the cleric, fuzzy hair decided to exit the mosque via the backyard corridor. Two low voltage bulbs illuminated either end of the passageway. The rest lay in relative darkness. A stiff breeze created a myriad of eerie sounds. The hoot of an owl sounded like the mournful cry of a distressed soul. He sauntered along lost in his own thoughts. He noticed movement in the corner of his eye. Fuzzy hair quickly stepped aside in a bid to counter the attack. He felt a painful punch in the ribs. The attacker pinned him against the stone wall. The force of the impact left him fighting to remain conscious. 'Do as I say or you will die here.' Fuzzy hair recognised the voice and decided not to resist. Rahim and fuzzy hair exited the mosque unseen. They drove straight to Khan's mansion. Rahim led his prisoner to the rear end of the mansion. He questioned fuzzy hair about his presence in the club. Fuzzy hair found he was in a no win situation. If he remained mum, Rahim would beat him to a pulp. If he spoke, the imam would have him exterminated. Hesitantly he spilt the beans. Fuzzy hair directed Rahim to the imam's secret warehouse. They recovered a sizable part of the arms and ammunition.

CHAPTER 6

Gautam's dedication and diligence propelled him to a senior managerial level in less than two years. A dispute between Hindus and Muslims over a tract of land in Kashmir threatened to erupt into a bloody battle. The Hindus claimed that a temple honouring Lord Shiva existed centuries before the Muslims came to India. They demanded permission to build a new temple. The Muslims claimed that a marble mausoleum had stood on the plot of land. The Muslims accused the Hindus of dismantling the tomb. The Muslim league insisted the plot be returned to them. After much coaxing, they managed to bring the two factions to the negotiating table. Gautam was chosen as one of the arbitrators. The matter dragged on for two years. Frustrated and annoyed Gautam suggested that the property be equally divided. The Muslims took umbrage. They said that the majority of Kashmiris were Muslims therefore the plot should be allotted to them. Gautam refused relent. A Muslim separatist group placed a price on Gautam's head. The central government ordered the police commissionaire to protect Gautam at all costs. The commissionaire of police made several unsuccessful attempts to smuggle his charge out of the valley.

Gautam was transferred to a safe house. In the wee hours of the morning two men stole into the property and sprayed the bedroom window with bullets. Gautam rolled off the bed and hid under it. The two men were gunned down by the security police. The commissionaire concluded that someone from within had informed the separatists of Gautam's bedroom. The following day they received a note warning that Gautam would only be permitted to leave Kashmir in a body bag. Gautam's life would remain under threat as long as he was in Kashmir. The commissionaire consulted a friend in the army. The friend advised that Gautam would be safest under the protection of the border security force. The separatists avoid the border area.

CHAPTER 7

The sight of the imam leaving in a Daimler rattled the cleric. The imam was only one who could stand up to Khan. Once he earned the imam's confidence, he could manipulate the grumpy old man. When the cleric learnt of the imam's return to the mosque, he rushed to greet him. The cleric stopped dead in his stride. The imam had about him the look of a hungry tiger. His cold steely eyes burned with rage. The incensed imam marched into his room and slammed the door shut behind him. The cleric was overjoyed. The meeting with Khan had ended badly. He believed the iron was hot enough to strike. The cleric knocked gently on the imam's door and waited for permission to enter. He asked if there was anything he could do for the imam. The imam asked for the head of Khan on a platter. The imam explained that when he first conceived the idea of Womb, Khan was the only one willing to provide finance. Once he got his hands on the statue, Khan would be eliminated. The cleric could hardly believe his ears. The imam was singing his song. All he needed to do now was to fan the flames of animosity. Once the imam assumed control, it would not take much to rid himself of the doddering old fool. He would declare himself the supreme leader of Womb. He would have the world call him "The Caliph". He imagined ways he could eliminate Khan. All he needed was an expert sniper. Salim would be his best bet. But Salim and Rahim were like two peas in a pod. He decided to first deal with Rahim. The cleric schemed several ways to kill Rahim. Every idea raised its own problems. It occurred to him that he should try and steal the statue on his own. He knew it was in Khan's safe. Several members of Khan's staff were corrupt. He wasted no time in contacting Ahmed, Khan's private accountant. He asked if Ahmed could open the safe. The accountant demanded a thousand rupees for the job. After intense bargaining, they settled at six hundred.

Ahmed waited for Khan to leave town. The cleric surreptitiously slipped into the mansion. They entered the office after lunch. The wife and the domestic staff had retired for a siesta. Ahmed's nerves were fully stretched. His hands shook like tuning forks as he attempted to open the safe. They were dumbfounded when they found the statue not there.

On his return, Khan noticed several fresh scratches around the lock. Khan was certain someone had tried to open it. He suspected the evil imam. He summoned Rahim to the mansion. He ordered his trusted confidant to take the statue to a remote military post on the Kashmir border. Ali would accompany him. The commanding officer was a childhood friend. He told Rahim to return immediately. Ali would remain at the post with the statue. The youngster must swear to guard the statue with his life. Khan cautioned that they must be wary once they enter the region of Pakistan occupied Kashmir. The imam was the undisputed king of that area. He gave them names and addresses of persons who would assist them if the need arose.

CHAPTER 8

Rahim and Ali drove out of Lahore at the crack of dawn in Khan's old Chevy. Besides the usual stopovers for food; the call of nature and refuelling, they drove more or less nonstop. Early evening they reached the outskirts of Pakistan occupied Kashmir. Trucks, taxis and private vehicles waited at the border. Rahim noticed some of the drivers surreptitiously pass money to the inspectors. The rest were subjected to close scrutiny. Rahim's car arrived at the check post booth. Two guards stuck their heads in through the front windows like curious macaques. Their hands hovered close to their pistols. The officer in charge approached the car. His face was as pockmarked as the surface of the moon. A prominent scar over his left brow marred his rugged good looks. He ordered Rahim to park the vehicle on the shoulder of the road and step out. Rahim handed the officer a letter written by Khan. The two line missive strictly forbade any harassment. The officer in charge's attitude changed instantly. He was aware of Khan's influence in the army and government. The imam's influence remained within the province. The millionaire could have him sacked. Rahim and Ali waited in his office while the officer phoned Lucknow. It took an hour to secure a connection. The chief apologised profusely for the delay. During the conversation, the chief repeatedly used the term sir. Rahim guessed he was talking to Khan. He would not dare refer to the imam as sir. They were guided past the other vehicles. After tea, snacks and refuelling they were well on the way to the border. The mighty Himalayas rose majestically around them. It was an awe inspiring sight. Rahim expertly manoeuvred the car over steep gradients and sharp bends. Clouds of thick fog hampered his vision. Switching on the headlights only made matters worse. At times Rahim was forced to crane his neck out of the window. At other times he stopped and waited for the fog to dissipate. About halfway up, Ali noticed Rahim constantly glance at the rear view mirror. He increased his speed. They were hurtling through a wall of thick mist at breakneck speed. Rahim had noticed a vehicle suddenly appear out of nowhere. He feared they were heading into an ambush. He ordered Ali to load his rifle and stay alert. The old Chevrolet rolled and pitched over the uneven surface. It fishtailed dangerously on sharp bends. The Ford on their tail was gaining on them. He told Ali to brace himself before slamming down the brakes. The nose of the Chevrolet dipped, it fishtailed violently, skidded out of control and rammed into a tree. Rahim and Ali jumped out while the car was still in motion. The Ford hit the rear end of the Chevrolet. The sound of metal ramming metal and splintering glass reverberated in the still silence of the woods, like the crescendo of a Wagnerian opera. Ali and Rahim sprinted into the safety of the woods. The deafening sound died away. They saw no movement of men inside the Ford. Rahim silently crept to the Chevy to retrieve the statue. Ali made his way to the Ford. A fountain of steam rose out of the radiator like a geyser. The bumper had fallen off and the grill had caved into the engine. An assortment of car parts lay scattered all over the road. The driver of the Ford lay draped over the steering wheel like a ragdoll. The man in the front passenger seat lay lifeless with his head resting on the dashboard. The rear passengers were flung clean out of the doors. Both men lay dead. Rahim and Ali sat by the roadside to review their situation. They had no idea where they were, nor how far they were from their destination. Ali opined that the road must lead to the border. He had not noticed any forks or crossroads along the way. The Himalayan chill bit through their sweaters. They decided to continue on foot. The sound of an approaching vehicle urged them to dive for cover. The vehicle screeched to a stop at the sight of the accident. They surveyed the accident in the beam of a powerful searchlight. Then they aimed the powerful beam in their direction. Time and again the searchlight beam swept over Rahim and Ali. On one occasion the beam remained focused on a spot uncomfortably close to them. Rahim opened fire, blowing out the searchlight and killing the searchlight operator. The area was plunged into blinding darkness. Five torchlights came alive. They cautiously proceeded towards Rahim and Ali. Keeping to the shadows, Rahim and Ali waited till their pursuers were within range and opened fire. Cries of pain answered the assault. They jumped into the battered Chevy and cranked the engine. There was no response. A military vehicle arrived on the scene. Rahim and Ali were arrested and driven to the check post.

****

Colonel Malik was expecting the new arrivals. He welcomed the guests cordially. Rahim was offered accommodation reserved exclusively for V.I.P. guests. Ali was given a room in the senior officer's quarters. After a dreamless slumber, Rahim and Ali met in the officer's mess for lunch. Rahim appeared troubled. He was convinced his boss's life was in imminent danger. He decided to return to Lahore that very day. But Colonel Malik was dead set against it. He explained that the evil imam's influence extended all the way to within a few miles from the border post. Rahim would be killed well before the check post.

Rahim and Ali were enjoying a quiet evening on the porch of the mess. They noticed a young jawan continuously approach them. He addressed Ali by his first name. It surprised both of them. Ali stared blankly at the stranger. The jawan introduced himself as Wahid from Bombay. The years rolled back. Ali was a boy of six, playing with children in the slums. Ali threw his arm around his childhood friend. He introduced the friend to Rahim. Rahim cross questioned Wahid. Wahid said that he was an ordinary jawan. He felt it his duty to warn Ali that his life was at risk. A subedar Chowdry, who is an agent of an imam in Lahore, has been tasked with killing them. The subedar receives orders through a grocer who supplies essential items to the post. Rahim wondered if the jawan was also an agent of the imam. Under the current circumstances one could not be too careful. The warning could be a diversion.

A little before midnight Rahim visited Ali's room. He placed a duffel bag on Ali's bed and withdrew the statue. Ali stared wide eyed at the flawless piece of art. He made Ali swear on the soul of Gautam that he would guard the statue with his life. He instructed Ali to remain within the confines of the camp until such time Khan or he called for him. He must keep the duffel bag with him at all times, even in the toilet. He must carry arms twenty four seven.

Ali remained circumspect about Rahim's departure. He suggested Rahim confer with Wahid before leaping into danger. Ali found his childhood friend on guard duty at the entrance. An hour later Wahid arrived. He urged them to be quick. He dare not be found missing while on duty. They discussed Rahim's plan to leave for Lahore. Wahid said that leaving the post would pose no problems, but reaching Lahore was a different matter.

From within a few miles all the way to the check post the imam's men watch every square inch. He warned Rahim about the imminent dangers he would face. However his colleague Khalid knew someone who could get him safely across the check post. Khalid and he were Khan's men. In spite of that Rahim would have to pay for the services.

CHAPTER 9

The cleric was intrigued to learn that Rahim and Ali been absent from Khan's mansion for several days. Ali lived there and Rahim spent most of his time in that house. He rushed to inform the imam. The imam did not bat an eyelid. Instead he spoke of a banquet he was to attend the following day. The cleric was mystified.

Khan's mansion was a hub of frantic activity. Caterers, decorators and the mansion staff were busy with their chores. Colourful lights lent the estate a fairyland glow. Foreign dignitaries, Supreme Court judges, high level government officers, the top brass of the armed forces and Islamic heads were among the invitees. The evil imam was one of them. Khan wished to make his son's birthday an event that would be spoken of for years to come. He decided to check with the caterers before he washed and dressed. He hurried down a long dimly lit passage that led to the servant's quarters and the backyard. That is where the food was being prepared. As he passed the storeroom, the door flew open. An arm shot out, grabbed him by his shirt sleeve and violently pulled him in. A wad of chloroform covered his nose and mouth. In a few seconds Khan passed out cold. He was bound, and gagged. A slimly built bespectacled man stepped out of the storeroom and made his way to the backyard. The bespectacled man's station wagon was parked near the delivery vans. No one paid him the slightest notice. A man collided with the bespectacled man and deftly slipped a piece of paper in his hand. The note instructed the bespectacled man to deliver Khan to a particular address. It was signed by the evil imam.

Expensive cars eased into the front gate. The guests were surprised by Khan's absence. Security men scoured the length and breadth of the mansion. The bespectacled man waited till the passageway was quiet and empty. He had Khan wrapped in a large hessian cloth bag. He dumped Khan into the station wagon and pulled out the gate, unimpeded. They travelled for the better part of the night to reach their destination. The cleric and six others waited for them in a small wooden structure in a wooded area. Khan was bound hand and foot and placed on an upright chair. The treatment of icy cold water and several cups of coffee revived the abductee. Hours later the imam arrived on the scene. He sat a few feet away from Khan. 'We can do this the painful way or the amicable way, the choice is yours.' Khan did not reply. The cleric was surprised by the prisoner's calmness. The imam asked where he had hidden the statue. 'Don't worry it is in safe hands' Khan mumbled.

'I am not in the least bit worried, but you should be. I believe one of the safe hands lies dead somewhere in the foothills of the Himalayas.'

'There are others.'

The imam decided to up the ante. The Bespectacled man lifted Khan's forefinger nail with a pair of pliers. Khan screamed and passed out. When he came to, his finger pulsated with unbearable pain. But he knew he was winning the battle. The imam was getting frustrated. 'Just shoot off his kneecaps' the cleric suggested. The imam played his trump card. Khan's wife and his nine year old son were ushered into the room. Khan's wife took one look at her roughed up husband and flew into a rage. She shouted insults at the imam. Khan was taken aback. He had never seen this side of his wife before. The son appeared confused. He had known the imam since he was a toddler. He could make nothing of the scene before him.

Khan was gripped with mind numbing fear. He helplessly gaped at them. 'So what's it going to be, the statue or the lives of your wife and son?' Khan did not speak for a long while. He took time to contemplate the matter. After careful consideration he decided not to relinquish the statue. His son was safe. He was the blue eyed boy of the most highly respected and influential imam in all of Pakistan. If he harmed the boy, the imam would be referred to as the late evil imam. The imam was baffled by Khan's decision. He sat seeped in deep thought. His threat had failed. He decided to s end the mother and child home. He warned them against speaking of this to anyone. The cleric could scarcely believe his ears. The imam's decision left him in a state of high anxiety. He reminded the imam that powerful people visit the mansion every day. A mere hint will have the mosque swarming with policemen.

The imam was furious. After the wife and child had left, he issued orders to shoot Khan and leave his body in the woods for the animals to eat. The cleric begged for the pleasure of executing the object of his hate. He snatched the gun from a guard.

The cleric walked up to Khan like a villain in a mafia movie. The sight of Khan bound and helpless gladdened his heart. 'So mister lord and master of all I survey, do tell how it feels now that the tables have turned? 'I warned you not to tangle with me, but you refused to listen. I tried to din it into your head that I am Allah's chosen one, but you scoffed at me. Well, here I am, on my way to becoming the leader of the Islamic world. And there you are, bound like a sacrificial goat.' The final insult ended in a crescendo. 'Now tell me where you have hidden the statue and I may spare your life? Tell me or your misery will continue till you drop dead' the cleric yelled. 'You are a fool. If I die I cannot tell you, and if I live I will not tell you. So go ahead and do your worst.'

'Where is the damn statue?' the cleric bellowed in frustration. Khan merely looked at his captor. 'Remember, I am not as weak willed as the imam. I will bring your wife and child back and torture them to death in your presence.' The cleric slapped Khan across the face; wrapped his bony fingers round his neck and hissed 'Were you fated to live long enough, you would have known the terror I can strike in the hearts of men.'

Khan shrugged his shoulders. 'I can do nothing, my hands are tied.' A guard standing by the cleric chuckled at the clever play of words. In a fit of blind rage, the cleric shot one of Khan's kneecaps. Khan let out a blood curdling cry of pain. A pall of silence fell on the room. The cleric paced the floor like an epileptic patient. His plan to retrieve the statue; kill Khan and the imam and declare himself the undisputed leader of womb was falling by the wayside. The guard could not bear to see Khan suffer. He forcefully retrieved the gun from the cleric and shot Khan between the eyes. He threw Khan over his shoulder and carried his body into the woods.

CHAPTER 10

Ali watched with misgivings as Rahim and the guide disappeared into bowels of the forest. Their progress over the uneven terrain was slow. They made their way up dangerously steep climbs and down precarious slopes. The guide warned of dacoits in the area. Rahim remained unfazed. They reached a village in the early hours of the morning. The guide led Rahim through a maze of narrow gullies. Rahim was introduced to a portly man in his sixties. The man's demeanour changed after he received his fees. They were given tea, snacks and a place to spend the night. At the crack of dawn, the portly man's son took Rahim to the village bus stop. The bus would take him to the town's bus depot. From there Rahim would need to change busses for Lahore. The conductor of the Lahore bus was their man. He would take care of him. Rahim suffered tense moments as a check post guard boarded the bus and questioned the passengers. The conductor tactfully distracted the guard as he approached Rahim.

From Lahore bus depot Rahim hired a taxi and headed straight for the mansion. He could tell at a glance that something was not right. Nothing was as it should be. Rahim's worst fears were being realised. He knew the evil imam was up to no good. He would need to be in top shape to enter the den of demons. He went home and passed out cold.

Around teatime Rahim left for the mosque armed to the teeth. He entered the congregation hall as silent as a cat. He used the backyard corridor to reach the imam's lair. He would need to go through an informal sitting room and past the dining room to reach the evil imam's lair. The imam's guards were enjoying a leisurely moment on the veranda of the sitting room. Rahim ran the risk of being spotted. He silently crept across the sitting room and stopped at the imam's door. The cleric's high pitched squeaky voice pierced the thick teak door. He could hear other voices in there. They were having a heated argument. One of the voices had a very familiar ring to it. The familiar voice was trying to convince the others he was one of them. The imam said he was pleased to know that, but insisted on knowing the statue's hiding place. The familiar voice denied any knowledge of a statue. He suggested they should ask his father. The imam replied in a matter of fact manner that his father was dead. When the familiar voice asked for the imam's leave, he was denied permission. The revelation, that Khan was dead depressed and angered Rahim. He finally recognised the man behind the familiar voice. It was Khan's eldest son Gulam. The lad was slightly built. He would be no match for the imam's roughens. Rahim had failed to save his boss. He felt it his solemn duty to do all he could for his master's offspring.

Rahim knew the son would be kept alive until the statue was found. The imam always had armed guards standing behind him when he was in a meeting. Rahim barged into the chamber and shot both the guards. The conversation came to an abrupt end. Everyone gaped unbelievingly at the gate crasher. It took a while for Rahim's presence to sink in. The imam could scarcely believe his eyes. His men had reported Rahim as dead. The cleric sat petrified with fear. Khan's son was relieved to see Rahim. The imam's veiled threats had made him wary. Rahim could not afford to procrastinate. The guards on the veranda barged into the room. They found Rahim holding a gun at the imam's head. They stopped dead in their tracks.

Rahim ordered the cleric to sit cross legged at the imam's feet. He threatened the others with the imam's death if they disobeyed his orders. He ordered the guards to leave their weapons on the floor and wait on the veranda. Rahim marched the imam, the cleric and the son towards the entrance of the mosque. Khan's son was told to lead the way. In the congregation hall, they were confronted by fuzzy hair and six others. Fuzzy hair's presence surprised Rahim. Not too long ago he had sworn allegiance to Khan. All six of fuzzy hair's men had their weapons aimed directly at Rahim and the son. Rahim cocked the revolver and moved between fuzzy hair and the son. 'Make your move and make my day' Rahim growled threateningly. 'A twitch from any of you and the imam dies.' Fuzzy hair's men held their ground, believing they had created a stalemate. The imam nerves gave way. 'Are you bloody deaf or demented?' Lay down your weapons and do exactly as he says.' Rahim ordered all of them to lie face down and stretch their limbs as far out as they could. He kicked the guns across the room. They backed towards the entrance in the order of the son, Rahim, the imam and the cleric. Suddenly the hall reverberated with a single shot of gunfire. Rahim arched his back and sank to the floor. The next two to fall were the imam and the cleric. The two men of God lay dead side by side. Fuzzy hair stood and saluted his new boss.

The guards were asked to gather in the hall. Khan's son stood before them, a picture of confidence. He declared himself supreme commander of womb. He instructed them to refer to him as Sherkhan. He warned he would be far more fearsome than Kipling's character from Jungle Book. He offered them the choice to serve him or leave. Of the twenty five men, fourteen volunteered to serve the new ruler. He had the loyalists march the others to the backyard at gunpoint. Moments later eleven bodies lay lifeless in the unkempt backyard.

Sherkhan offered a sizable reward for anyone who could furnish credible information about Ali. One of the men informed him that Ali was sent to a border post in Pakistan occupied Kashmir. The man had no idea which border post it could be. Sherkhan recalled that the imam had an army of loyal followers in area. Someone from among the thousands of sycophants was bound to know.

****

The imam had decreed he was to be buried in his hometown. The imam's followers from all over Pakistan attended the funeral. Shops, restaurants and other businesses had respectfully downed their shutters. Sherkhan and fuzzy hair attended the funeral. The police had informed the mourners that the aging imam had died of heart failure. The police chief sensed tension in the air. Suddenly all hell broke loose. The crowds demanded that the perpetrator be arrested without delay. The police quelled the threatening outbreak with assurances that it was just a rumour. Sherkhan and fuzzy hair searched for someone who knew of the precise border post. They happened to run into man who supplied goods to the border post. Sherkhan and fuzzy hair and a group of armed men arrived at the border post. Sherkhan believed he had all his pawns exactly where he wanted them. In his mind success was a foregone conclusion.

CHAPTER 11

Gautam enjoyed life in the Himalayas. The grandeur and majesty of the range left him enthralled. He could not get enough of it. The slender silver-grey trees added to the breath taking beauty of the landscape. He could now appreciate why the Himalayas were regarded as the abode of the Gods. All he needed was Padmini by his side.

Soon boredom set in. Gautam repeatedly requested for permission to join the daily patrols. Finally the commander agreed. On one of the trips they found themselves under heavy fire from across enemy lines. More than half of the men were killed. Poor visibility hampered an appropriate counter offensive. Besides, there were too few of them. The radio was another casualty of enemy fire. Gautam became a liability. It placed the chief in a quandary. It was imperative that he contact the base camp for reinforcements. Gautam volunteered to walk to the base camp. He argued that he was not much use to them as a combatant. Besides, the base camp was less than an hour's walk away. All he needed to do was follow the border fence. Reluctantly the chief agreed.

Halfway into his trek the weather changed for the worse. Gautam felt like a blind man in unfamiliar surroundings. He stopped to assess his situation. His strong sense of duty urged him to continue. The lives of four men depended on him. Heavy laden clouds obliterated the moon and stars. There were no indications to guide him in the right direction. The barbed wire fence too had mysteriously disappeared. He could not recall any steep gradients on their journey from the base camp. He was forced to accept that he was lost. Halfway up the hill, Gautam found a large rock that offered adequate shelter from the piercing wind. He fought his way to it and decided to wait for Mother Nature to calm down.

The morning brought with it some relief. Gautam felt hungry, drowsy, stiff and too numb to move. For miles around the snow had carpeted the earth. He struggled to stand and look around. All he saw was miles of snow covered hillsides. The valley seemed to have disappeared. He decided to stay put and hope for the best. Either his Goddess would come to his aid or he was destined for a snowy grave.

The distinct crack of a gunshot penetrated the chill morning air. He noticed a hazy figure scrambling downhill. He was too weak and hungry to even signal his presence.

CHAPTER 12

Word of the events at the mosque reached training camp. Tuglaq feared for Ali's safety. He slipped away from the camp and headed for Lahore. An employee of Khan revealed the location of the border post. Tuglaq caught the first bus to Pakistan occupied Kashmir. A bus conductor helped him catch a bus to a village. From there a guide escorted him through the woods to the border post.

No news from Rahim worried Ali. He kept himself occupied with physical exercises and combat training. He explored the immediate surroundings in the event he needed to flee. A security guard informed him that he had a visitor from Lahore. The sight of Tuglaq was a shock. He wore the unmistakable expression of one bearing ill tidings. Tuglaq wasted no time in informing Ali of the tragedy. He went on to reveal that Khan's son had assumed the name of Sherkhan and declared himself supreme leader of Womb. He warned that he was coming after Ali. Alarm bells rang in Ali's head. He had little doubt that Sherkhan was after the statue. Out of the blue, Vikram dropped in. He advised Ali and Tuglaq to flee. He warned that Ali's evening meal drugged. Some people were coming to take him back to Lahore. After a final handshake, he hurried away.

Ali sat and contemplated his next move. The bison flatly refused to leave his side. He decided to spend the night in the woods. Ali packed two thick woollen sweaters, tin foods, water, binoculars, a pistol and numerous rounds of ammunition. They navigated their way to the secret hideout. Ali waited till he had a good look at the mysterious Sherkhan. He planned to return and eke revenge. Around lunchtime, the guests arrived. Ali recognised fuzzy hair instantly. The pompous one had to be Sherkhan. He appeared disturbed and angry for some reason. The chief was at pains to calm him. They made their way to the forests. They searched high and low, often coming within a few feet of the hideout. As soon as they left, he and Tuglaq scampered away. They started their decent down the precipitous slope. Ali swept the hillsides with his field glasses. A lone figure appeared in sight. Ali studied the lone stranger's movements. The fellow was apparently unarmed. His every step seemed laboured. The unfortunate man appeared to be at the end of his tether. He seemed to struggle just to stay upright. Moments later Ali saw him stagger and collapse. Initially Ali decided to ignore the unlucky victim of the Himalayas. But something deep within, urged him to go to his aid. Tuglaq vociferously disagreed. Their argument was interrupted by a gunshot. Tuglaq emitted a low gurgling sound and collapsed in the snow. Ali was torn between loyalty and self-preservation. Another report of gunfire urged him to flee the scene.

Ali reached the hapless stranger. At a single glance he could tell that the man was suffering from hunger and exposure. He poured hot tea down the stranger's throat and fed him some baked beans. The man revived faster than Ali expected. But his speech was slurred and his limbs continued to shake. Ali offered the man the spare sweater. The man ignored the kind gesture. He gaped wide eyed at Ali's arm and almost imperceptibly spoke his name. Ali stared at the stranger in disbelief. The stranger pointed to Ali's arm. The gesture said it all. Ali knew of only one man who could recognise the scar. For the moment the pursuers were forgotten. They hugged and laughed senselessly.

Ali handed Gautam the duffel bag. Gautam gaped unbelievingly at the contents. He was speechless. Their joyous reunion was marred by the sound of voices behind them. Ali turned and saw a band of armed men shimming down the slope. Ali and Gautam fled like they were pursued by Lucifer. A hail of bullets followed them all the way. A twenty feet cliff stopped them in their strides. Ali wondered if Gautam could manage it. Not even death could persuade Ali to leave Gautam's side again. There was no time to procrastinate. Their pursuers were gaining ground on them. The bullets were nearing their mark. It wouldn't be long before the band of killers would reach the cliff. The two friends leapt off the side, trusting in Gautam's Goddess. They landed on a bed of soft snow. Briefly they celebrated their victory. An ominous rumbling sound disrupted their moment of joy. The rumbling morphed into a deafening roar. A white monster chased after them at breakneck speed. It felled trees and pushed huge boulders out of the way. The monster hit them with the power of a runaway train. It engulfed them in its bosom and carried on unperturbed. The white monster stopped when it reached the base of the hill. Still silence fell like a shroud over the hillside. The Himalayas towered majestically over the world, unmoved by recent events. An eagle soared overhead. The Goddess had fulfilled her objective. The two souls were finally together in the great beyond.

THE END

THIS BOOK IS DEDICATED TO MY EMOTIONALLY ADOPTED SON KIRAN. HE URGED ME TO CONTINUE WRITING, IN SPITE OF MY LACK OF SELF-CONFIDENCE. I THANK MY GOD AND HIM FOR HELPING ME TO STAY FOCUS